HOW TO FIND WHAT ISN'T LOST

A SHORT, PRO-INTELLECTUAL, PRO-DESIRE
GUIDE TO ENLIGHTENMENT

AKILESH AYYAR

SIFTING PRESS

For more information about the ideas in this book, visit

Sifting to the Truth

http://www.siftingtothetruth.com/

To my teachers

CONTENTS

PREFACE

This book has a simple, single purpose: to help you awaken to your true nature. I provide the spiritual system that I developed to help myself. It is itself based on the Hindu mystical school of Vedanta, along with other ideas from both literature, psychoanalysis, and philosophy.

Most importantly, I have drawn from experience.

The world is unsatisfactory. You can't control it, and at best, even if you attain what you want, it is always tainted by the specter of losing it, and of your death and the death of those you love. Ultimate meaning seems incomprehensible. Why are we here and what is the point?

The idea of enlightenment is that there is a way to perfect, lasting happiness and meaning beyond the seeming constraints of this world. In fact, it contends that this happiness and meaning is nothing other than what you already are.

You have mistaken yourself for a body and a mind — this sounds bizarre, even crazy, I know, but it is the truth — and as a result suffer from their limitations. This mistake can be corrected. We experience dualistically, through the division between "me" and "everything that's not me," but the truth is non-dual.

The theory section of this book will in large part be devoted to working out how and why this is a plausible picture of reality. Both philosophical considerations and the experiences of the wise over history and in various cultures support it.

The Self (that is, our true one, as opposed to the normal, everyday person we think we are) is pure, uninterrupted being, awareness, and bliss, and it is beyond all limitations. It is not any particular awareness or consciousness. It is that out of which all particular consciousness arises.

Enlightenment means to realize this fact not as an abstract set of words but in experience.

Enlightenment is and is not religious. It is religious in the sense that it suggests that there is something very important beyond what we know with our senses and mind. It is not religious in that it requires no blind belief in God, prayer, sacrifice, scripture, or membership in any church: merely a willingness to look deeply into your experience of yourself. It is self-validating. Anyone can test it and experience it for themselves.

I could tell you that enlightenment will make you less selfish and help you save the world. This might happen, because it will release you from a large number of negative emotions. The reality, though, is that it may or may not lead to greater service and charity.

Enlightenment is peace and joy, but not in the normal sense of those words. Its peace and joy is perfectly compatible, in a strange way, with ordinary pain and suffering. Enlightenment reveals that there is no world and that there are no people, at least not in the way you think there are. So saving the world may or may not happen then. To proceed into the inner mysteries, you have to be willing to give up prior notions, assumptions, and goals. To enter the temple sanctum, you have to remove your shoes and bow your head.

Trust me, it's worth it.

Enlightenment is not just for mystics in a mountain cave. It is something available to everyone, because it is your nature right now. Something stops you from recognizing what you are literally experiencing this second and at all times.

It takes no special talent to get to that recognition, only a sense that there is something more and a strong desire to obtain it.

I know this to be true for a fact. You can find my personal spiritual experience at the back of this book, though if you are new to the non-dualistic way of thinking (or even if you aren't), you might get more out of it after reading the rest of the book.

This book is meant to be short, dense, and useful. Its purpose is to help you attain a goal that, I have to say — in classic paradoxical spiritual teacher fashion — is not a goal, and cannot be attained. And yet you must try with all your strength and sincerity to attain it.

I hope for this book to be a simple tool just sufficient to

the task: rough, ready, and made to accomplish, not to dazzle.

Let me also make a couple of important disclaimers. I thought hard about how to make this book flow as organically as possible, and banged my head against that problem until I realized that it was a variant of the perfectionism that I'd always suffered.

Perfectionism isn't entirely bad. It is actually a pointer to the spirit, where alone real perfection lies. Perfection isn't to be obtained in the realm of action and result. That isn't to say that effort and quality don't matter — far from it. But *in particular* when working on that which deals with the spirit, there is a special problem with trying to make something perfect. Perfection in art and engineering usually involves full comprehension, full seeing, and then translation of that seeing into a work. That's miraculously hard when it comes to even the "normal world," but it becomes downright impossible when it comes to the depths of the soul. There, words stumble and turn back, perplexed and befuddled. Mind cannot penetrate: and where mind cannot penetrate, what hope is there of consciously attained perfection? Perfection will come if it comes by the choice of a higher power.

In the meanwhile, I'll go by the maxim that the perfect is the enemy of the good, and good is what I hope for this book to be. In the meantime, I apologize in advance for those places where I stumble and fall.

I'd also love to hear your thoughts on the book and your spiritual journey. If you want to let me know how you feel, have questions, or perhaps want to learn more closely from me, feel free to contact me at my website, Sifting to the Truth:

http://www.siftingtothetruth.com/
I look forward to hearing from you.
Good journeying.

INTRODUCTION: THE BIG PICTURE

The basic case this book makes is simple. It is that at heart, what you seek in life, whatever else you may say or think, is to know your own self, or Self, in its typical spiritual capitalization.

The Self is bliss, peace, happiness, meaning, and truth, though not quite in the way in which you understand these terms. The Self will resolve the most cutting of your existential worries, will assuage your fears of death, will console you for your losses and your disappointments, will reassure you always.

And — it — is — what — you — are — right — now.

You just don't know it. Or you sort of know it, but not quite in the right way.

Something like that.

Still, be assured that it is what you have been seeking, and what you already are. Is it a paradox to seek what you already are? If so, it is one of many paradoxes to come.

We'll call this clear experience of the Self enlightenment. It could also be called self-realization, moksha, nirvana, or liberation.

Now there is good reason to believe that there is a way to see this truth clearly, not just intellectually (though the intellect is very important), but in your own experience. When you do, you will understand why all the benefits promised above are in essence true, even if they are somewhat imprecise when worded that way.

There is very little talk of God in this book. Belief in God is not required to proceed, though neither is it disregarded. In essence, the question of God is an individual one, and belief either way is compatible with the route to the Self outlined here.

The Self, it is true, is not just something in the physical world. It is something special, something which will quite literally blow your mind. But it is also true that it is not the conventional concept of God. Precisely what it is can and will be described, but it is in truth beyond words. In the end, it can only be experienced.

The system in this book is derived from a few main sources. The first is that Hindu school of mysticism called Advaita Vedanta, in which I was initially educated by my teacher, Swami Bodhananda Saraswati. This book's ideas owe their deepest debt to that most sublime genius of Vedanta, Sri Ramana Maharshi.

The other main sources of this book include other mystic traditions, and certain key authors and ideas in literature (the work of the stupendous French novelist Marcel Proust in particular), Western philosophy (in particular the long debate about the relationship between mind and body), and psychoanalysis (the work of Freud and his successors). I've learned a great deal about the last from my own psychoanalysis, which has been, thanks to the tireless work of my analyst, a profound growing experience all its own.

The essential method in this book is three-fold, deriving again from a Vedantic conception of spiritual education.

The first step is to learn the intellectual theory. I'll explain why there is good reason to believe that the enlightenment experience exists, that it is desirable, and that you personally can achieve it. For many, this will depend on showing why the scientific worldview, while very useful, cannot explain it all, and especially cannot explain human consciousness. The exact relationship between the Self and the mind will also be explored, and this too will be part of a good road map. Importantly, I'll also explain why the path to enlightenment depends crucially on two more activities: quieting the mind and the pursuit of the Self.

Second, I'll explain the method to quiet the mind. A quiet mind means one in which disturbing thoughts are infrequent and mild. A quiet mind is capable of deep focus. To quiet the mind, you must get more and more honest about your true desires, and pursue them one way or the other. This requires openness to and expression of your feelings and desires, and a progressive testing of them to understand their meaning. Self-discovery is an organic process of opening and blooming. You will also have to resolve your intellectual doubts about the whole arena of spirituality. This takes time.

The most important means of quieting the mind is one which requires a certain amount of quietness to use. It is

also the third step of the system: what I call the pursuit of
the Self. A quiet mind is relatively quiet; the Self when
pursued and recognized shows you always to have been
Quietness itself. This pursuit consists of two activities: self-
inquiry and surrender, and culminates in the seeing
through of the illusion of personal identity.

Actually all three of the steps are inseparable. Knowledge quiets the mind. A quiet mind absorbs knowledge
better. Knowledge is required for the pursuit of the Self, but
that pursuit also increases one's knowledge. A quiet mind
helps in the pursuit of the Self, and that pursuit quiets
the mind.

In fact, every section and chapter is shot through with all
three steps.

So these are all self-reinforcing components of a single
thing. I am only separating them for ease of use.

**How this book is different from other spiritual ideas and
systems**

The general thrust of the spiritual scene today falls into one
of two camps: the traditional or the "New Age." Both of
these categories, of course, cover systems with vast
differences.

Still, I'd like to make some **ridiculously stereotypical
and imprecise generalizations.**

The traditions, on the good side tend to be:

- Embedded in a strong institutional structure and
  community

- Time-tested
- Knowledgeable about a body of scripture
- Mostly respectful of the intellect

Unfortunately they also tend to be:

- Rigid and hierarchical: open mainly to an elite
- Not open to new views
- Unnecessarily obscure
- Often repressive of desire

New Age systems, on the other hand, are praiseworthy because they:

- Are compassionate, accepting, and non-judgmental
- Keep things simple and accessible to the masses

On the other hand they often:

- Are oversimplistic
- Dismiss the value of the intellect
- Are sappy and sentimental
- Pay little attention to emotional preparation
- Have overly indulgent ideas about desire

Both the traditions and the New Age philosophies usually have a fairly one-note idea of how to deal with problems of motivation and negative emotion. When I say problems of motivation, I am talking about conflicts with wanting to do what you "know" you should do. It's the kind of issue you might have when you know you're "supposed to" get up in the morning and run, but don't want to, or when you know you should stop smoking and you don't. It encompasses all kinds of self-destructive behavior. As for negative emotions, I mean the obvious: feelings like anger, sadness, regret, guilt, etc.

The usual recommendation in nearly every case boils down to one of a few options: simply allow yourself to be aware of the problem without any judgment; take some simple practical step; remember some key bit of philosophical knowledge ("I am one with everything"); or give yourself a pep talk ("if not now, when?").

These are indeed useful insights, and they all have their place, but by themselves they are woefully inadequate for most people. Moreover, they are lost opportunities.

I'm obviously biased by what helped me, but I believe neither of these camps has it right. First, unlike most in the New Age camp, I think the intellect needs to be respected and allowed full questioning and a wide range. For the seeker, it is a great tool of independent thinking, of checking to see whether something makes sense and is not bullshit. It provides a road map and yields an important, if limited, understanding of things. It is the ladder by which one climbs an important segment of the mountain. The intellect's demands to understand are to be satisfied to the greatest extent possible; when they are, the intellect itself will recognize that there are realities that are beyond its ken.

And to that end, I have tried to provide as much relevant philosophy as I could in this short book.

The other key point is the need for much greater psychological sophistication than either side offers. The knowledge that psychoanalysis has discovered over the century since Freud about unconscious, inner conflict is to be treasured. Emotional growth and insight are crucial to spiritual growth and insight. There is also the immense power of artistic and literary expression to heal pain, discern the real meaning of desire, and most of all, to discover beauty of our individual viewpoints. All these quiet the mind. The investigation and expression of the individual self is not at war with the recognition of the true Self. The first is required for the second. All these points have too often been neglected by the two camps.

Deep-seated issues need to be addressed by some combination of psychoanalytic psychotherapy (contact your local psychoanalytic institute for a referral) with a trained therapist and an artistic-philosophical approach to experience that includes methods I call "metaphorization" and "the science of desire." In all cases, there is an investigation into the meaning and messages which these feelings are trying to communicate.

The "science of desire" takes desire — by which I simply mean what we want — very seriously. Desire is not, as in the traditions, viewed as something to be repressed. Nor is it, however, as in many New Age systems, simply something to be indulged or dissolved with some spiritual magic wand.

Not everything in the mind can be explained and handled using purely spiritual methods. And reaching the end of the spiritual journey does not solve all mental and emotional problems, though it helps.

Desire and negative emotions need to be listened to and

unfolded. If they are intense, they are not merely to be "loved away" or "accepted" or disappeared with positive thinking and silence. They are not to be shrugged off or squelched. They carry at least two messages. One is about needs we have that we are not satisfying or being honest about. The second is the inner beauty of our own unique minds and perspectives, which we can extract and enjoy through a process of artistic expression. That expression is itself a need we must fulfill, just as we must eat and drink to pursue the spiritual quest.

Unlike the traditional systems, I don't believe in the need for any repression of desire or emphasis on "willpower." Rather, all it takes is to listen to and express our feelings, and *they will moderate themselves*. Sometimes motivational problems or negative emotions arise because they point to knowledge or perspectives we have but are not noticing. When we notice them and give them a voice, they integrate into our lives in a more peaceful way.

So the key difference between my system and most other spiritual systems is this joint emphasis on the importance of the intellect and the importance of exploring the messages within desire and emotion.

Think for yourself

One more note. Every person's circumstances differ. Every person's temperament and background differs. Think for yourself. No teacher or teaching is to be idolized: they are but pointers and paths and maps, not the destination. They are all flawed.

Take my teaching, but with a critical mind: evaluate it to

see if it is effective in your own life, and, if necessary, adjust it.

The sincere seeker finds the right teacher and the right path. Sincerity simply means that you actually do want more happiness and truth than the world offers, and that you exert relentless effort over time to find it.

PART I

LEARN THE THEORY

1

WHY BELIEVE IN ENLIGHTENMENT?

I'm going to start by explaining why we think enlightenment as an experience would exist. I'm going to give these arguments in fairly short form here.

The first key point, given our culture, is to destabilize the idea, branded into the mind of most educated people today, that the scientific investigation of the physical world is going to be able to solve everything. Science is, and, by its nature, will *always* be inadequate to explain the great existential mysteries. No technological advance or discovery will ever alter this fact. I explain why below.

IT IS a truism to say that science works miracles. Over the centuries, and in particular over the 19th and 20th centuries, it has created vaccines, space ships, the Internet, nuclear power, the internal combustion engine, mass flight, and much more. So it is not surprising that scientists are the high priests of our day: we turn to them for answers, and expect that one day, any mystery still undisclosed will be disclosed. Where once there was darkness, science will shed light.

The truth is that while science has indeed been terribly productive, its productivity has been limited to certain specific arenas, and it has never gone beyond them. Its inherent strengths necessarily bind it, and the very lights it can shine on some things render others invisible.

Science cannot give us the meaning of our lives; it cannot fully explain us to ourselves; it cannot tell us what the true basis of reality is. To understand why, we need to see just what science is.

Science is about the testable

Science is a method of organizing observations about things into concepts, and making testable predictions based upon those concepts. We see, hear, touch, see, and feel, either using our naked senses, or aided by certain instruments. Based on that data, we hypothesize patterns about the way nature works, and we test those hypotheses by collecting more data. If the new data matches our hypotheses, that strengthens our beliefs that they are correct – that is, that they are permanent features of the world that describe it accurately.

To take a famous example in the history of science, we observe swans. We notice that they are all white. We hypothesize that all swans are white. And then we keep observing swans. For a long time, the data might match our hypothesis. What to do, then, on the day we see our first black swan? Time to change the hypothesis. (And in fact, there really are black swans.)

So collect data, hypothesize, test, and, potentially, revise hypothesis: that's the scientific method.

And we take our hypotheses and build them into greater and greater structures. Science is a search for order. We want to see our patterns combined with each other into great cathedrals of patterns. We do not just want a random hypothesis here and there, but prefer laws that show how great patterns of patterns work. That is, for example, the power of concepts like natural selection or gravity. They serve as the bulwark for whole multitudes of patterns. Yet they, too, are ultimately subject to testing.

Science's great power, its shield against becoming a rigid dogma, is the power of its hypothesized patterns to be tested, and to be tested with sense data. In theory, anyone with access to the right situation and instruments can observe with their senses what previous scientists have observed, and see if the data actually match the hypotheses and theories.

OF COURSE, this is an idealized version of science. There are in practice several deviations.

In fact, for example, anomalies are ignored all the time. When people look for a pattern in data – say, they test an equation for the weather against the actual trend – there are always at least slight disparities between what is expected and what is observed.

The question is how these deviations should be dealt with. Are they merely outliers, random noise in the data that is irrelevant, or perhaps artifacts of the statistical procedures used, or of errors in the instruments? If they are, they should be dismissed; their existence should not affect our belief in the patterns they are supposed to test.

If, on the other hand, these deviations are not outliers but are correct, then even one deviation invalidates the hypothesis. How is a scientist to choose between these possibilities? The data itself cannot tell him. It is a judgment call, and it happens based on the scientist's other values. Inevitably, it happens for human reasons. For example, a small piece of data that seems on its surface to violate the law of gravity will be dismissed as an outlier, an artifact of some problem in the procedure. This is because to invalidate the law of gravity based on this one piece of data would throw physics into chaos. So the scientist invalidates the data instead! Is this strictly speaking "scientific"? It is – but it shows the value choices that go into science. Science, despite its virtue of testability, is not at its core driven by tests. Human choice drives it.

Hypotheses which are more central to our beliefs as a whole, that is, which serve as foundations for other hypotheses, are less likely to be abandoned even when data contradict them. Instead, some auxiliary hypothesis that is also involved in the test is more likely to be changed or invalidated ("it's not gravity that's wrong, it's our notion of the composition of the rocks involved in this test."). Or perhaps the testing instrument will be considered to be malfunctioning ("should have fixed the computer better").

Another component of that human choice is intuition. We often have a picture of scientists looking objectively at the data and then coming up with new hypotheses. In fact, science most often works in reverse. Scientists come up with hypotheses based off of intuition and then look for just the data that might test those hypotheses. Intuition plays a grand role in the development of science.

And this intuition is even more critical because, for any particular set of data, no matter how large, an infinite number of patterns may be generated from it. For example, to take a somewhat silly example, one could, as an alternative to the law of gravity, hypothesize that for the first 20 billion years of the universe's existence gravity holds, and then that it doesn't. This is equally consistent with the data. When it is tested, it comes out equally unscathed. Another possibility: things move completely randomly; it's just that everything has coincidentally moved in a pattern that looks exactly as if gravity existed, but that could all change at any instant.

So why don't we regard these alternatives as valid hypothesis? It is not because the data show them to be wrong. The data do not contradict them. We consider them wrong for other reasons, the specifics of which are matters of controversy. One possibility is that there's a heuristic rule that we should pick the simpler rule over the more complex wherever possible. This is known as Ockham's razor, after the English earl who invented it. Yet there is no scientific reason to believe it is true, since there is no way to test it. The very definition of our problem is that more than one hypothesis – of more than one shade of complexity – matches the data – and so we can never test Ockham's razor against data.

Moreover, Ockham's razor does not actually solve our problem. To think that everything is random is definitely simpler than the law of gravity. Gravity brings in all kinds of equations; the idea of randomness does not.

Yet of course the hypothesis that the universe is random does not seem strictly testable. It is just possible that randomness would yield something that looks like order. A coin flipped a hundred times *could* show heads-tails-heads-tails all the way to the end. And in fact, that particular pattern would be no more or less likely than any other. Yet if any amount of seeming order is deemed compatible with randomness, what would be the way, in principle, to test it?

There is no way in principle to test it, because any result might in theory be compatible with it, might seem randomly generated. This then might be deemed not a scientific hypothesis at all. Yet gravity is actually in the same predicament. Even if data showed things flying up and down for no obvious reason, we could either say gravity is an incorrect concept, or we could hypothesize a new force that is actually in effect and working against gravity.

In that sense, gravity is theoretically immune from refutation. If one wants, one can always invent a reason why the data do not affect it – the data are outliers; the instruments are wrong; another concept or force is at work.

So data can never fully explain scientific concepts despite the centrality of testability. Predictive power cannot do it either, since that too becomes a human judgment. *Do* the data show that a particular theory makes accurate predictions or not? There is no clear rule by which this can be judged.

This seems to violate our intuitions. It seems like science is less arbitrary than this. And it might be, if we assume certain things about the human mind.

If we assume that the universe is orderly and that our minds are adapted to finding this order; if we assume that the concepts we come up with are not coincidental, and that our intuitions are not purely subjective, but bear some fundamental relationship to the universe – science becomes less arbitrary. We have to assume that the universe is perfectly suited to be found out by human minds, that it consists of patterns precisely built for their excavation and articulation by scientists.

The biggest fundamental assumption here is what is called induction, and the philosopher David Hume outlined the problem of it in the 19th century. Induction is the idea that we can examine a certain set of observations in the world and generalize to the rest. We see 100 swans, not all of them, and then extrapolate to the rest. We observe how DNA works in 1000 people, not in everyone on the planet, and generalize to the rest.

To put it another way, we are generalizing from observations made in the past to observations we shall make in the future.

Why is this generalization a problem? It is a problem if science prides itself on being exclusively a matter of logic and not of faith. What reason, after all, asked Hume, do we have for believing that the past has *any* relationship to the future, that the very method of looking at the past to predict the future has any basis at all?

The only reason given is that the method has worked in the past. Yet this falls into a trap. Taking from the fact that the method has worked in the past – and using that as evidence that the method will work in the future – is itself *an example* of the very method in question. The previous "successes" of science have exactly zero bearing on the future utility of science unless one has already assumed that the past bears on the future, and that induction works. Induction works because – induction works? That is what is called a circular argument.

What we must conclude is that science works on a great deal of unjustified intuition and faith. This is not to say that these are wrong. It's simply to recognize the truth behind the method. Science assumes an orderly world, inductively knowable, built for the intuitive capacities of the human mind to conceptualize.

Nor are these merely theoretical or academic matters. Take a current-day controversy raging in the halls of physics: the validity of string theory. This theory holds, in short and distorted summary, that the universe is made of tiny strings that are plucked, the vibrations from which create the universe.

In *The Trouble with Physics*, physicist Lee Smolin points out that the very elegance of the mathematical equations in string theory, the elegance that permits them to harmonize many other patterns in physics and arrange them into a cohesive whole, prevents string theory from being adequately tested. So here the scientific virtue of elegance and orderliness in the universe and the scientific virtue of testability are pitted directly against one another. Of course it is possible that one day string theory shall become more testable – but it is not clear when that shall happen. How shall scientists judge this conflict?

Now all these reservations about science aside, it nevertheless remains the most testable mode of knowledge discovery. That is its virtue. Despite all the possible ways to game the system, still in theory any hypothesis is testable with reference to data that in theory any human with senses intact can obtain. That is, the data is "public."

This public testability gives science a huge advantage over rival systems of knowledge acquisition like religion, which rely on other sources of authority, like private experience or scripture.

Unfortunately, public testability comes at a steep price. Testability requires drawing a line and saying – this thing either happened or it didn't. It fell along this side of the line or on the other side of it. There is no half-pregnant. And that kind of judgment, in turn, requires translating any observation into, essentially, a number. The observation has to become measurable. And when it has become measurable, then it may be compared against the measurement that was predicted.

And the public nature of this measurement means a sharp reliance on the senses to the exclusion of other sources and kinds of experiences.

Together, these make science an extraordinarily powerful tool for investigating those realms that are basically composed of public sense data that are well-suited to measurement, and an extraordinarily poor tool for those realms that are not. Unfortunately, our most mysterious realms are of this second kind.

We're going to go on a rapid voyage through the lands where science cannot effectively tread.

Science can tell us what is, but not what should be.

Science can predict the workings of much of the world, but it cannot tell us what we should make of it, what we should do with it.

The "should" here is not something that we can test or measure out there. It is not publicly available for the senses. It is not merely what the majority of people *say* should happen. It is a conclusion of our own considered reflective sense. Beyond that, entire fields of philosophy, religion, and literature have been devoted to questions of the "should." But science cannot solve it directly.

Science might tell us that one action will help life and

another will help death, but why should we value life over death? That, science cannot tell us.

People talk all the time about how science has made inroads into fields previously thought impervious to it. Yet science has never made one single tiny inroad into this "should," because its conclusions simply do not speak to it. Might as well be upset that a jar of peanut butter can't play jazz saxophone.

Indeed, science cannot even say what *in science* is worth investigating next. Of all the topics a scientist might approach – which one next, and why? This is not purely a scientific question. It depends on what the scientist values, and science itself can say nothing about what a scientist should value. It can speak only to the consequences of each possible choice.

Science can deal with the measurable but not the immeasurable

Science is used to numerical comparison. Yet all the concepts, emotions, and values that we place most highly cannot be reduced to numbers. How can love or freedom be reduced to a number?

Values cannot be reduced to numbers. Feelings in all their richness and complexity cannot be reduced to numbers. Words cannot be reduced to numbers – at least not in a way that preserves their integrity.

Measuring anything keeps some of it and dispenses with the rest. Yet when dealing with the core of our internal world, to dispense with any portion of it is to destroy it.

Science deals with causes but not reasons

More importantly, science cannot explain human action in terms that satisfy us. We crave an understanding of ourselves that preserves ourselves, in our own eyes, as free beings. We do not want to see ourselves as clockwork automatons, and no view of science that paints us in this light will ultimately be satisfying. And we are all looking for those concepts that will satisfy us. It is this satisfaction that we take to be the marker of truth. Even in science, as we saw above, satisfaction is as close to a marker of truth as we can get.

Science explains in terms of cause-effect relationships, in terms of mechanism. This data triggers this pattern, which spits out that data. When applied to human beings, this makes us out to be robots. Now many people do in fact deeply believe humans to be simply robots, but these people are not, by and large, the spiritual seekers. And in fact, even those who do believe that do not really treat themselves or their loved ones as if they were robots. They treat them as if they were free beings.

Science cannot explain why there is something rather than nothing.

Important philosophers from Gottfried Leibniz to William James have called the question of why there is something at all rather than nothing the Great Question.

Science by its nature cannot answer this question. It can

only arrange data into patterns. It cannot explain *why* the data exist *at all*. That would require something beyond sense data to feed into it as cause. Yet the data of science can only come from the senses. Move beyond the senses and you lose the things that make science science, like the public nature of the data and its testability.

So science is locked into assuming things as they are, and it does not have the tools to coherently pose or answer the question of why things are. Yet this is a question at the core of human life.

Science cannot explain consciousness

Perhaps the most important domain into which science, try as it may, cannot trespass, concerns the status of consciousness. It's a well-known question among academic philosophers, but not among the educated public.

In academic philosophy, the experiences we have – the redness of a rose, the smell of fresh coffee, the feeling of anger – are called "qualia." If we are nothing but physical mechanisms, qualia must be explicable in physical terms.

Only if they were explicable in physical terms would they be accessible to the kind of public testing that science requires. And if they were not so explicable, then they would constitute a domain that science could not enter. This has serious implications, because for science to be the grand framework, capable of answering our deepest questions, it must be able to explain a phenomenon as omnipresent as our consciousness.

Yet it cannot. To show you why, let's do a simple thought experiment. Philosophers love thought experiments. This experiment is not of my invention, but is known in the philosophical literature as "spectrum inversion."

Imagine that where you saw the color white, I saw the color black, and vice-versa, and so on for every color. Importantly, though, we both called things by the same names and acted towards them in the same way. In other words, we both called a cucumber "green" and the sky "blue," ate one and flew kites in the other. Would we ever be able to tell that our colors were reversed in this way? No.

Because try as anyone might to examine our bodies or brains, they could never find out, by looking at cell activity, what color each of us saw in our private mental movie theater, what it is *like* for each of us to have a particular experience. There is a fundamental disconnect between what brain cells or chemicals look like and the colors we see. Where in the brain is the color red? Dissect away to your heart's content: you will never find it. That redness takes place in our minds, in our private domains.

Indeed, even if a machine existed that supposedly read from neurons what color another person was seeing and displayed it on a monitor — how would anyone tell if it were accurate? Someone would have to observe the monitor. Their own colors might be reversed. No one could ever know if the monitor were calibrated correctly. No amount of physical observation with even the most sophisticated physical instruments would solve this problem. My mind allows me to experience things, but by that same nature bars me from directly knowing the experiences of others.

The fact of our perceiving switched colors would remain forever unknown. The thought experiment shows that scientism, which holds that everything there is can be understood by the scientific examination of the physical

world, cannot explain what it is like to have an experience –
which is the most fundamental, everyday thing there is!

The basic responses of the scientistic philosophers to
these arguments fall into two categories. Some claim that
qualia are an illusion – that we literally do not experience
them at all, but only talk as if we do. There is no "inner
movie" playing in front of you right now; you do not see
these words in some space in your mind. These are just
misleading words, they claim. To call our most intimate
experience illusory sounds like gibberish to me. It's even
more so because usually illusion is in reference to some true
reality — for example, the lake in a mirage might turn out to
be just sand. But when we talk about experience itself, the
illusion *is* the thing to be explained. Just the fact that we
experience at all is what has to be accounted for. So the
whole argument rings of desperation.

Others argue that science has not yet but will someday
show the physical basis for qualia, even though we cannot
conceive how, because science solves everything. This is just
blind faith, of course, since science has not solved everything. As already mentioned, it has never said what is good
and evil, for example. And it never will. It can tell us facts,
but not what to value.

Similarly, it is not only currently impossible for science
to explain qualia, it will remain forever so, because there is
an impassable conceptual hurdle in its way. As we saw
above, scientists will always have minds themselves, their
own qualia machines, which will prevent them from ever
entering anyone else's mind. That means the subject of a
mind can never be made public knowledge in the way that
science requires. And that means the scientistic worldview
is inherently limited; not everything in human experience
can be explained by examining the mechanisms of phys-

ical matter. Evolution cannot hope to fully explain conscious experience as an adaptation. Computer scientists are unlikely to produce awareness mechanically, since it is not merely a question of assembling physical materials.

What does all this signify? If consciousness can never be fully explained by science, it means that there is a realm of personal, private truth which must be investigated by other means. The way is cleared for art, meditation, spirituality, and introspection, devalued in recent years, as alternative and necessary paths to truth—not just personal growth, but *truth*.

Don't get me wrong. Science should proceed and make what headway it can to understand the human condition. It only has no right to foreclose as irrational or archaic those private paths of truth-seeking that human kind always has, and always must, continue to pursue, each person ultimately looking within.

NOW WE CAN DRAW two conclusions from the failure of science to explain consciousness: a strong one and a weak one.

The strong one goes like this. There there has to be an substance underlying the changes in the world. Many people today believe that substance to be matter, and matter alone. Matter explains a lot, but it doesn't explain the most fundamental thing there is: our own experience of the world and of ourselves, what it's like to be us. Our inner movie.

So another possibility is that there is another substance, a kind of awareness-substance or experience-substance, that explains these things. Now, we could then posit that matter and awareness exist as co-substances underlying change. This is a position called dualism.

The problem with dualism is this: how do these two completely different substances interact to create the world and our experiences? They are fundamentally different, so they can't touch. If they interacted, they could only do it because they are each parts of some other, third substance. Then that substance would be the truly fundamental one.

So dualism doesn't work. Now consider one more possibility. Could awareness as a substance explain everything in the material world? It could, of course. We only know the material world *through* our awareness, after all.

So the underlying substance could be awareness, not matter at all. All matter could just be seen as thoughts in that awareness. Now I don't mean that individual awareness would be that substance. I mean some kind of universal awareness-**substance** which would hold all our individual awarenesses as well as the world within it. That would explain both matter and our experience perfectly well. So what's the difference between that universal awareness-substance and matter? The difference is that awareness is, well, aware. It's — alive. It's sentient.

The cosmic mind exists. It is the Self.

So if the substance underlying the universe is not dead matter but sentient awareness, then what are we? That substance would be a cosmic mind, so we as individuals would be thoughts within it. But if our minds, our identities, are merely those thoughts, then what we are in *reality* — our permanent unchanging state — is not those individual minds, but that permanent cosmic awareness, that underlying mind.

What we are in permanent reality — is that not a phrase that simply describes our actual, true self?

And that is precisely what enlightenment aims to show us is true. We are actually nothing other or less than that cosmic mind, which is the only Self any of us has. And this is not just philosophical speculation. We can experience this fact.

∾

The weaker conclusion: take it as a useful assumption

Now if you don't buy this conclusion, a weaker conclusion will do the trick nearly as well. The point is that matter doesn't explain everything. Even if an awareness-substance doesn't underlie the universe, the point is that scientific investigation, which is based purely on matter, cannot account for everything.

Which means that there is good reason to start investigating other ways of knowing. And that openness to these other ways is all that's required to proceed. There is indeed a direct way of knowing reality, and whatever we call it, the experience of it remains the same. A rose by any other name and all.

That said, it is very useful as a spiritual seeker to take the assumption of a cosmic mind as *provisionally true*, whether or not it actually "is" true. It serves as a good road map to guide the practical steps you will need to take to have your own experience, upon which you can make your own judgment. So we are going to take it as true for the sake of this book.

Enlightenment is plausible because of the experiences of the wise over time

We've opened up the possibility of other ways of knowing and suggested the philosophical plausibility of a universal awareness which is our true Self and of the personal experience of this fact. There is another valid source for this belief: the personal experiences of the wise over time and throughout various cultures.

Aldous Huxley in his excellent book *The Perennial Philosophy*, itself a perennial topic of debate in the religious studies academy, suggests that all the religions have one face for the masses, and another face for the few who are interested in esoteric, mystical truth. And Huxley, after examining them, suggests that in every religion, the mystical ideas are in fundamental agreement.

Though the facades may differ, there is a common core. Joseph Campbell, the great comparative mythologist, said much the same thing.

The wise in all these traditions have affirmed through their personal experiences that there is a way to a higher knowledge not subject to the usual uncertainties, and that this is the heart of truth, happiness, goodness, and meaning. The mystical schools of Vedanta in Hinduism, Sufism in Islam, the Pseudo-Dionysians and Gnostics in Christianity, many schools in Buddhism and Taoism generally, and the Kabbalah in Judaism all illustrate this.

The sages and prophets and mystics have spoken and written about their experiences, and they seem to agree that there is a source of ultimate truth and being beyond the mind and that there is a path to personal experiences of it. Beyond that, the exact steps suggested vary and the descriptions of what is attained vary as well.

The important thing to keep in mind is the widespread agreement that there is Something More, that there are ways to know it for yourself, and that it is ultimately beyond words. So take a path to it that resonates with you — this book describes one such path — and then you can judge for yourself how it should best be described.

2

THE RELATIONSHIP BETWEEN SELF AND MIND

Some possible relationships between self and Self

Last chapter we established our reasons for believing in a Self which is also a pure consciousness, a cosmic mind. What is the relationship, exactly, between the Self and our individual minds? This is a great mystery, and there is no perfect answer to it. Not even enlightenment reveals that answer; it transcends the question.

For seekers, however, it can be very useful to try to comprehend this relationship intellectually to some extent, as it can help guide their practice and quiet their intellectual desire to understand.

So in this chapter, when I refer to you and me, I am referring to our individual minds and bodies, our identities as separate people, not our true identities as the Self. But this relative, provisional level of knowledge is required as a seeker.

So IF IN and through everything is a pure, unbroken and eternal consciousness – what does that make you and me?

It makes us thoughts, among other things. And the next question must be: what impact does that have on our quest? In order to understand the answer to that, we have to look into what it would mean for us to be a thought in the mind of something inconceivably great, something beyond all thinkable limitations.

In envisioning something strange and new, analogies can be helpful. We feel we understand something fully only when we can put an image to it, when we have captured it in a kind of static picture that we can draw from in the future.

What we are trying to understand is the relationship between our very sense of being separate selves and the idea that behind ourselves and reality, and streaming through every pore of it, constituting it, is not matter but pure consciousness.

What is this sense of being separate? When we awaken from deep sleep, many authors, philosophers, and artists have observed that there might be a moment when we don't even know who we are. Then the memories and identity descend on us like a mask, or, more accurately, like a face.

In fact, even in that moment of not knowing who we are, that mask of identity has already started to descend. That is the mask that allows us to say "I" – that differentiates for us between what is "in here" and therefore part of ourselves from what is "out there" and therefore not-us.

Great thinkers like Gandhi and Einstein have pointed out the significance of this identity function. For we extend our identity, at least loosely, to those we love. We include within it, at least to some extent, our friends and family, our community, and those we perceive to share our values. They are us. And we extend to this community of identity some of the same love we give ourselves, the same benefits of the doubt, and the same desire to protect and nurture and nourish – and sometimes the same desire to destroy. Morality is different inside this circle of identification than outside. This is of course the origin of the idea of tribalism; morality applies within the tribe, not outside it.

This identity or ego thought is also at the center of our notion of spirituality. We mistakenly identify ourselves with our bodies and our particular minds. If we systematically investigate that identification, it loosens, and we realize that we are not in fact our bodies and minds.

But what *is* that identity which we observe, then, and what is its significance? Why are we seeing it, and why have we been deceived into thinking it is us? For the place of our limited mindset, our particular tiny perspective, in the greater whole, we look to analogies.

We are not looking for an image or conception that is going to be the absolute truth. The absolute truth lies in enlightenment. Rather, we are regarding our own desire for understanding as a desire for a set of ideas that will satisfy it when carefully considered, just as hunger is a need for a set of materials that will satisfy it when eaten. It is for this purpose that we turn to various analogies, to see if they can shed some light.

≈

Life as a dream

The first analogy, and one long used in eastern philosophy, is that of the dreamer and the dream. "Am I a king dreaming of being a butterfly, or a butterfly dreaming of being a king?" asked the ancient Chinese philosopher Zhuangzi. The

Hindus thought their god Vishnu dreamed the universe. And across the East the idea of enlightenment is equated with the idea of awakening.

In a dream, the dreamer can believe she is any kind of character or even several characters, even ones unrelated to his real life or completely fantastical. The dreamer imagines herself to be inside some particular dream character's body, or can see herself as an impersonal perspective. The laws of logic or even of physics do not apply in dreams, and time and space can bend backwards and forwards.

One way of thinking about ourselves is that we are dreaming right now. In other words, the person we think ourselves to be is actually a dream character. We are actually the dreamer who imagines himself to be a particular person. This is what the movie *Inception* was all about – the possibility that life might simply be a dream, and that if it were, we would not be able to tell if we were in the dream or in waking reality. The philosopher Descartes famously pondered the question of how we might know if everything in life was not completely a dream made up by a demon (his unsatisfying answer was that God wouldn't permit such deception).

One problem with comparing our situation to a dream is the illogic of dreams. Dream material is mostly stolen and mixed-up bits of real life, often colored by psychological motivations. Dream creation is an unconscious, primitive process, influenced by our memories as well by the way our body feels during sleep, including sounds we may hear and pains we may experience. Yet the world around us appears to be exquisitely logical and intricate, far more rational and stable than the typical dream.

Dreams also assume the possibility of waking into a realm that is ultimately much like the dream realm. Yet we are seeking an analogy with a crucial difference. If we awoke out of this dream, we would be waking not just out of the dream but out of our selves. Our very sense of identity, the very sense that we are separate people: that is what is dreamt. What would be beyond that would of course then be nothing like that we could conceive. It would not simply be a more logical version of the dream reality. It would be a reality where identities did not exist as we know them at all.

Finally, dreams are solipsistic. Dreams assume that there is only one character. We as the dreamer inhabit that character; everyone else is a figment of our imagination. Of course we as the dream character do not know what it is like to be the dreamer. That is alien and beyond our scope of knowledge. Still, it seems to be troubling that no one but us exists in this analogy.

Still, let us keep it on hand as we try another.

Life as The Matrix

The Matrix suggested another kind of possibility: that all of reality is an illusion, and that everything is computer-generated. In *The Matrix*, evil computers took over the world and kept humans in tanks in which they were fed on like batteries. To keep them docile in these tanks, it broadcasted pleasant dreams of a decent but certainly not perfect world that they could live in. That invented world was called the Matrix. These humans would live and die, completely ignorant of the unreality of their lives, within a perfectly-simulated imaginary world while their real bodies were in fact being slowly sipped like milkshakes by monstrous machines. In this world, Keanu Reeves' character Neo, one such enslaved human, meets a secret, underground resistance bent on escaping the Matrix and eventually ending it. Morpheus, the leader of the resistance, offers him a choice: Neo can take a red pill and exit the Matrix and enter the real world, or he can take the blue pill and stay in it, kept mercifully away from the bitter truth. The real world is hellish and uncertain compared to the relatively normal life that Neo enjoys in the Matrix. The movie poses this possibility as a challenge, again, to our sense of reality. How do we know we are not in the Matrix right now, and what would it mean to take the red pill?

The Matrix's world is far more logical and tightly-built than a dream, and the things in it work according to the laws of physics and science as they seem to do in our own reality. Its world, unlike in the dream analogy, is deliberately made. It reflects design and thought, not merely the psychologically arranged residues of life. That does seem to better match some of the ideas we have on the table.

It is not, however, enough to completely fit our sense of our situation.

First, the Matrix only generates the physical scenery in its world. It does not generate the other people in the Matrix, except of course for the ubiquitous agents which carry out its cleanup tasks and fight Neo in massive bullet-dodging action scenes. Yet we are looking for an explanation of people, of consciousness, and of the mind, not just of the inanimate objects in the world. The Matrix is not a good analogy for these.

Second, The Matrix again falls into the dream problem of creating a true reality which is too much like its fabricated world. The true reality outside the Matrix follows the same basic physical laws as the world within the Matrix, and has the same kinds of human beings in it – it is simply more desolate and rubble-strewn than the world inside the Matrix.

Yet in our investigation, we need to understand something considerably more mysterious than merely a more depressing, dystopian version of our own world. Whatever is outside our particular minds has got to be different than the world as we see it: not merely different in degree, but radically different. It would not be a "world" as we knew it at all, because it would not include our identities, our sense of being separate entities.

Life as The Truman Show

Contrast *The Matrix* to an earlier predecessor with a similar theme, the underrated masterpiece *The Truman Show*. In *The Truman Show*, Jim Carrey's character Truman Burbank lives in a world in which he is watched 24 hours a day by a TV cast and crew. He is, like the people in *The Matrix*, blissfully ignorant of that fact. His entire town and society is a film façade, his neighbors are actors, and everything is put together for the benefit of the television-watching audience. This is of course the idea of reality television taken to its logical extreme.

Truman eventually discovers the ruse, and at the end of the movie, we see him stepping beyond and into the real world.

One interesting idea that *The Truman Show* puts forth is that our lives may be a kind of art. Truman isn't in his show because he is being secretly devoured by malevolent supercomputers. He is in his show because millions of people outside it love watching him and his antics. The director creates the entire scenario for the interests of art, for his viewers' pleasure and for his own creative enjoyment.

That is an interesting new twist to our analogies. No longer are we looking at the feverish psychology of the body that generates dreams or the computer-generated dystopia that simply hypnotizes people with its vision. Now we are seeing a world built for the enjoyment of spectators, a vision created for a kind of beauty, however unethical.

Yet *The Truman Show* again suffers from the same problems the other two analogies had: the real world that it seems to offer, what little we see and know of it, is not too different from the world that Truman inhabits. It's much larger and much less happy, since Truman lives in an artificial utopia, but it's still peopled by people and it still works according to the laws of physics. It is still a world where Truman retains his mind.

Can we imagine a world where that mind is stripped away entirely? We of course cannot imagine it, at least, not directly. We can only venture certain speculations about it; we cannot picture it. If we could picture it, it would be physical, and it would be like our world. Yet we are still nevertheless heroically trying to create a picture of the unpicturable.

Also, it is not just the façade of the world and its bit players that we are trying to place as thoughts in the great mind behind everything. It is our entire beings. It is not just that we are seeing different things than in reality, but that sight itself, awareness itself, things themselves, only exist to us. They could not exist in the Real World, or if they did, they would be items beyond perspective, unimaginable items, viewable by creatures without limited minds. We are not merely changing glasses and we are not merely changing the scenery. We are asking what we might see if we did not need eyes or a limited mind to see at all.

The lesson to be learned from *The Truman Show* is that it seems to suggest a very interesting purpose to the world: the world, and our very identities, may exist in order to be experienced, in order to be seen, in order to be enjoyed. And this makes beautiful sense of our limitations. For the very fact that we are restricted to a particular sense of self and to a particular perspective – that we identify with our bodies and our particular thoughts, that we can see and know and do only so much and no more – also means that the world is focused in just such a way. Of all the ways to see the world, only each individual person, as limited as a single tiny keyhole in a universe-sized door, can see the world in their particular fashion, from their particular angle. If there were an audience that was without those limits, that very unlimited quality would *itself* be a kind of limit. They might enjoy, therefore, seeing what limits are like. As great artists have observed, art is born from constriction and restriction. That is what prompts resourcefulness, creates suspense, and lays the foundation for beauty. Our minds may be the way that something without limits can appreciate limitation.

Life as a novel

This brings us to another analogy: the relationship of an author to a character. A novelist writes up different characters, and in doing so, she also writes their minds. It is a very interesting situation, for in fact they have no reality nor any minds except when read by the author or another reader. The words that are written convey no significance except to one who already has the ability to translate those characters into mental concepts.

A character's mind does not actually exist. It is a reconstruction, a kind of optical illusion – similar to the way that the human eye actually only admits a little information at a time, but the brain and mind construct an entire image based on those few bits. Similarly, a character's mind is not actually on the page. Instead, from a few of the character's thoughts and actions as they are put down in words, the reader interprets and constructs a plausible mind, wears for a moment like a mask the character's perspective. And how does the reader know what the character's perspective must be? By reading the words, the reader automatically puts himself in the character's place and emulates the character's motions and thoughts, and so intuits what he would do in that character's circumstance and with that character's background. Literature, then, is a set of instructions for simulating other people's minds.

This gets us closer still to the proper analogy for our own mind. For our own thoughts are piped in every second into our mind, as are our sense perceptions. Could we be putting on our own personalities like a reader dons a character's mindset briefly? And here again the analogy breaks down a bit, because readers already have their own personalities, whereas presumably that which is beyond our own identity does not – or at least not in any way that we can conceive.

Still, the artistic design of the world and of ourselves, and also of the minimal information that is actually given in the world and from which so much must be interpreted and reconstructed all speak to the quality of this analogy. Another advantage it possesses over the previous analogies is that the character's mind is not of the same kind as the author's mind. The "real world" is totally different than the character: the character is merely a set of scribbles on a page; the real world is flesh and blood and three-dimensional. The characters do not even really have minds. They only seem to have them. In fact the very notion of a character is itself just an interpretation of the text. There is no character; there is only the reader and what happens in the reader's mind when the text impacts it. That kind of massive gap or chasm between the kind of person and world that is in fiction and the kind of person or world that is the author and the author's reality: it is that kind of chasm that we are trying to capture in our analogy. It is a radical difference of kind.

One problem with the author-fictional character analogy is that it is only about text. Images, sounds, smells, and touch are not accounted for – except as they are captured in text and simulated in the mind of the reader.

Life as a movie

So perhaps another, better analogy might be the relationship of a movie director to the characters in a movie. This sounds like *The Truman Show* again, but is isn't. In *The Truman Show*, Jim Carrey's character is real; his life is set up in a façade, but he is considered a real person. In this new analogy, I am not talking of us as being real people at all, but as being completely fictional characters. Just as Jim Carrey's character was a kind of guinea pig in the movie, in another sense his character, to us as audience of the movie, is purely fictional. Our relationship to his character, or the actual director or actor's relationship to the real movie *The Truman Show* (not the fictional TV show that the movie is about) – that is the kind of relationship I am talking about. There the director does not deal solely with text but also with sights and sounds.

The relationship of the character and the characters' world to the real world of the director and the actor is useful, and it does account for sights and sounds and other perceptions. There is, again, a radical difference between a wholly fictitious reality where even the thoughts are not completely laid out and the real world outside the movie. Inside the movie, everything is partial. It is a giant optical illusion.

And by whom is that illusion put together? It is ultimately reconstructed again, not in the reader this time, but in the viewer. The viewer receives 30 or more frames per second and hears the sounds and not only puts them together but imagines what is beyond those frames and sounds, constructs an entire world and fake people in it. And here there are subtle problems with both the novel and the movie analogies. Who is meant to be us in these analogies? The character – or the reader – or the author or director – or the actor?

Perhaps we are some of each of these. The author or director is after all the first reader or viewer. And reading and viewing again require simulating, or pretending to be, the characters that we read; and that of course is the first prerequisite of acting.

We must be first of all our characters at some level, but we are characters who do not know that they are being written, or that they are merely in a movie, that they are mere illusions, half-formed shadows with nothing behind them. At the same time, we must also be the audience that puts together the novel and the movie in our mind and appreciates them. Otherwise, the novel is just text and the movie is just strips of film or digital bytes.

And in and through all this we must also be part of that giant mind or consciousness which is creating all this. So in that sense we are again also the actor and director, though we do not know it and cannot see it for ourselves. We are the actor, the mask, the costume, the audience, the scenery, and the director. We are everything but can only know that abstractly.

And all this might make a movie a fine analogy for our situation, except that a movie is a static thing. It is not living. Once set, it is finished – created and kept, an object of the past.

Perhaps something which is more lively, which is being continuously created, would be a more apt comparison.

Life as theater

Which brings us to the theater. In a theater production, creation happens from moment to moment. There is also a script, with characters brought to life in an imaginary world. The director can deal with the full array of the senses, including touch and sight and even perhaps smell if so desired (another limitation, at least for the moment, of the movie analogy). Yet at the same time, there is a degree of improvisation to it. The actors are acting in real time, and every performance is different. Scripts are sometimes forgotten or altered, and the micro-tremulations of voice and gesture that so inform the portrayal of a character can be altered based on the actor's mood.

And the world outside the imaginary creation of the play is, again, radically different, since the characters in the play do not exist outside of it, nor does their world. They are creations of their script, made complete first by the actors who portray them and then by the audience who watches the entire production and can grasp it as a whole. So perhaps we are the characters portrayed by actors in a play, characters who do not know they are actors, of course, played by actors who do. And while the characters are doomed to live out the same lives day after day of the production, they are, by virtue of the acting and the direction, nevertheless also living out those same lives out just slightly differently each time.

Yet perhaps the theater still does not quite capture the improvisational quality of life, and also the sense that we cannot really penetrate into others' minds. There is an isolation we experience in real life combined with a freedom. We know our own mind, but can never figure out what another person is thinking, or if indeed they are thinking at all. There is a limited script, yet the very notion of the story may change – for the actors as well as for the characters.

Life as a video game

What form of art might portray this set of circumstances? One possibility is the video game – and in particular that peculiarly contemporary version of it called the Massively Multiplayer Online Roleplaying Game – or MMORPG. In this kind of game, players log into servers through their individual copies of the game and interact with other players in virtual worlds. These games usually revolve around some kind of fantasy, whether it be in Tolkien-esque middle age fantasy, space fantasy, or super hero fantasy.

This is a kind of "Matrix" where players play imaginary

characters. The characters, of course, do not know – or are not supposed to know – that they are imaginary, but the players, of course, know, and the boundary between the character and the player can be porous. The nature of reality is again totally different between the player's world and the character's world – the character's world is not photorealistic for starters. For another, what can be done is bounded by programming. Yet beside that element of the world that is scripted through computer code and rigidly repetitive, there is also an element that is human, as "non player characters," often members of the game development team, interject and shape elements of the story. At the same time, much of the game depends on what the players choose to do with each other: with the friendships and rivalries they develop between themselves, and how they react to the pre-programmed or pre-scheduled parts of the game.

No player communicates directly with any other player in the game: all players act only by going through a main server. Even if one player electronically chats with another, this communication goes through the server.

In this sense, the MMORPG is a model what the German philosopher and mathematician Gottfried Leibniz called a monadic world. Leibniz, who lived in the 17th century, invented calculus around the same time as Newton, but independently from him.

Monads were Leibniz's conception of how minds related to God. Each of us, he said, was a kind of pinpoint of aware-ness, an indivisible soul, that was given a vision of the world that we could interact with. This vision was given by God. Yet when we interacted with other people in that world, we never actually contacted them directly. Our little monadic minds only communicated our intentions to God, which modified the vision of the world he sent all the monads accordingly. There was no direct monad-to-monad communication. Everything went through God – or, in our case, the server.

What this captures accurately is the sense we have that though we are part of a greater consciousness that may be everything, still our feeling of isolation is complete. We really have no idea whether anyone else even really exists, and certainly have no idea whether they understand us when we speak to them. They might seem to understand us – but how do we know our words are really conveying to them what we think they are? After all, each person starts from a different context and perspective. Communication is an uncertain medium for conveying our inner experiences, and one which comes with no confirmation of receipt.

The problem with the video game analogy is that its limits are, like the Matrix, set sharply by the computer. It can do nothing a computer cannot do. The life of the imagination is severely curtailed by that restriction.

So THESE ARE the collected analogies for how the singular universal consciousness might relate to our individual minds and experiences: the dreamer to the dream, the world outside the Matrix to the world inside it, the world outside Truman's fake town to the world inside it, the novelist and readers to the novelist's created characters, movie creators and audiences to movie characters, theater artists and audiences to theater characters, and video game creators and players to video game characters.

None of these are complete. None of these are wholly accurate. All contain distortions. Yet all are suggestive. None can really account for the fact that our very identities and ability to experience at all are dependent on our minds, and the individuality of those minds, if stripped away, would yield a kind of reality we cannot conceive. And it is in that reality which we cannot conceive, that giant mind about which we can say little or nothing, that our own little minds are thought.

Yet from these analogies we can draw certain interesting possibilities. We do not know them to be true, but they help satisfy our need for philosophical meaning and for a better understanding of the game of enlightenment.

That relationship which we are curious about is beyond strange. Our little world might just be illogical and irrational compared to the 'real world.' It is plausibly a work of art created for the enjoyment of spectators – spectators which we may ourselves ultimately be. In this work of art, not only thoughts but feelings and sense perceptions are piped into our minds. In this work of art we may be isolated from the other players and characters, so that we cannot know them directly.

We do walk within a kind of virtual reality, and we cannot really hope to know the truth — *in the way in which we usually understand knowledge* — without giving up the very instrument with which we would know it. A character in a novel or a movie or a video game can never know that they are imaginary: it is the reader, the audience, or the player that can know that. The character that seems to know it is simply a changed thought in the player's mind. The character that seemed ignorant is now simply changed into a character that seems to know – but in both cases the character only seems to be ignorant or to know. The character has no independent existence. It is really the audience which appreciates the character and who brings both versions of it to life, that audience which must also at some level be a creative intelligence and artist.

We refer to that intelligence as an "it." We do not know its gender, we do not know its form. We do not even know that it is singular. The "it" may be plural. But we do know that there is an intelligence that we can regard as a sort of creator of the art form – the unique form, the one encompasses all the others – of our life experiences, and of our very identities.

This "it" must at some base level be *us*, because everything is part of the same consciousness – the only separations being in thought, the thoughts of that consciousness. At the same time, "it" cannot be us-as-minds-and-bodies because "it" is beyond limitation and we are quite clearly limited. This is a paradox that in the end we must resign ourselves to not fully being able to understand. Enlightenment brings not understanding but a going beyond the question. The exact magic trick by which the unknowable and unlimited turns itself into the seemingly knowable and limited can only be glimpsed from the corner of our eye, not seen clearly and directly.

We and "it" are separated by our identity, that is, by our very sense of limitation, powerlessness, and ignorance. As the character in a novel or a movie is powerless relative to the author or the director, so too are we similarly powerless even though we are inextricably connected.

And yet we do have one power, one unique ability: we have the power to see the world as only limited creatures can. Our perspectives shape our view, and perspectives are formed by their boundaries. Our identities as ourselves, complete with human forms and memories, vulnerabilities and flaws, and our exclusions of everyone beyond our small circle of friend and family and community from self-love: all this makes us ourselves. And it shapes the reality we see. No one but us can see things that way. If, as I have posited by analogy, it can be useful to think of our lives as art, that is the artistic purpose of our limitation.

Just as characters in a novel see the world in the way they see it precisely because of their blinders, and just as adults cannot see the world as children do exactly because adult knowledge prevents them, so too are we constructions of thought whose virtue is in our narrowness. Our limitations and our identities create our perspectives, and that makes perfect sense if we are art, just as the limited size of the canvas shapes the painting on it. Yet we must also keep in mind that we are art at only one level; at another we must be artist, and put together we are the audience as well.

Finally all the analogies break down, or rather, we must take them all for what they are worth. Each of them is flawed, like ourselves, and each, again like us, has its use.

If our minds are a kind of art for which we are the audience, and our own deeper selves, more alien that we can possibly imagine, sit on the other side of our perspectives, constantly creating us – is there a means of communication with It, this Artist behind the mind?

There is — it is called metaphorization. We will cover it later in the book. It will help us communicate with this Artist and uncover and explore our desires. This in turn will help us quiet our mind to the point that we can discover that in truth, we are the reality that lies beyond the duality of art and artist.

3

THE STRUCTURE OF ENLIGHTENMENT

The whole thing is very simple. You think you're a separate person: a body, a mind, a personality, with a mother and father and siblings and friends, an occupation, and a place in society. You think you have feelings and thoughts. You think you currently look out at the world. You have pleasures and pains, hopes and worries and dreams.

That's what you *think*. Actually, you are not this separate person. You are the pure consciousness in which this separate person manifests. This is the same pure consciousness, the same cosmic mind, which we've already discussed extensively.

This pure awareness is not a thing — "pure awareness" is just an approximation. What you actually are cannot be exactly stated. It is beyond all limits. It is beyond mortality, beyond love and hate, beyond past and present and future. It is even beyond awareness as we know it; pure awareness is what allows for normal awareness, but it also allows for normal *unawareness*, so it encompasses both. Similarly, it includes both being and non-being: so we can call it pure

Being, which is really something indescribable. It allows everything to manifest, but it is no specific thing. Its nature is peace, but it is not the peace that comes and goes. Its nature is presence, but it is not the presence that is opposed to absence. Its nature is awareness, but it is not the awareness that goes away when you are in deep sleep.

But this thing that you are is what you've been looking for. It is solid, it is permanent, it untouchable, it is immortal, it is absolutely perfect — so perfect that it includes within itself all modes of imperfection without itself being blemished. It is extraordinary. It is mind-blowing. It is unbelievable.

It is also something you are experiencing right here, right now. You are under the influence of a kind of optical illusion that makes you believe that you are this separate person with all its worries and cares. Free yourself of this illusion and you will see that what you really are cannot be touched by those worries and cares. They may still exist, but they will not belong to you — because "you" do not exist. Not in the way that you think you do.

It's hard to explain, obviously. What is beyond words is immediately shot through with strangeness and contradiction as soon as you try to speak or write about it. But this is the essence of enlightenment: seeing the true nature of reality, absolutely and beyond a doubt.

It does not solve all mysteries, but it solves the most crucial one: it allows you to know without a doubt that you are, now and forever, free and at home.

∾

Ignorance, Ego, Mirage, Mystery

So if we are experiencing our Self all the time, why don't we feel it? One word: ignorance. By this I don't mean ignorance in the normal sense. I mean a special quality of our mind that veils us from ourselves.

If we accept the cosmic mind hypothesis, then there is a pure consciousness out of which everything manifests. Whatever analogy we use to describe its relationship to its manifestations, there is another fundamental question relevant to our spiritual task. Just how is it that a Self that is a single and singular, pure consciousness creates minds which have lost their sense of being that cosmic mind? How does the cosmic mind forget what it itself is? If there is only that cosmic mind, how can it create something unaware of itself?

In one sense, this question is one of the eternal mysteries that remains even after enlightenment.

In another sense, however, it is critical to understanding the project of enlightenment and the way it proceeds. The truth is that at no time is the cosmic mind ever fooled.

What happens it that it becomes *aware of the thought of being unaware*, the *thought of forgetfulness*. In enlightenment, it becomes *aware of the thought of being aware*.

It is, to use yet another movie analogy, like someone (let's call her Anna) watching a movie of someone (let's call her Beatriz) watching a movie about a third person (let's call her Cat). Beatriz becomes so absorbed in Cat's story that she forgets she is just a spectator. Betty is terrified when Cat is terrified and thrilled when she is thrilled. At a certain point, when Cat is in mortal danger, perhaps, Betty suddenly remembers that she's not actually Cat, and that's she's sitting on a comfortable couch in complete safety.

In this analogy, Betty has just had a spiritual realization. But was Anna ever fooled? Not for one second.

So what afflicts Betty is what's being addressed. And is Betty real? Betty is not real. Betty is just an image. Betty is never "really" fooled either — she is just a character, a fictional entity. She cannot actually believe anything. She does not have real states of mind. But she appears to be fooled, and she appears to be enlightened, and both of those appearances actually happen in Anna's mind.

Of course, in truth, Anna is not a person — she is pure consciousness. She is just the space in which the movies within movies appear.

What hurts Betty we call ignorance, which is the appearance of being identified with a limited personality and body. Ignorance is itself an illusion, as we've seen, since it occurs to a fictional character, but to that character it seems totally real and hurtful, just as pain in a dream would seem real to a dream character, though the sleeper is never actually affected.

So how do we get rid of ignorance?

Ignorance is *identification* with the idea of being a particular person. The Self thinks the thought of a character which believes itself to be independent, a Pinocchio which is only a puppet, but which says — through the ventriloquism of the Self — that it is a real boy. Ignorance is the identification with the character, and that character *is* the identifying thought. They arise simultaneously, as two sides of the same coin. What we call the character *is* the construction of the *idea* of "a character" which believes itself to be real, and believes it experiences things and is in control of its own actions.

That idea, that ignorance, when examined carefully,

turns out to be completely incoherent. It vanishes upon inspection.

Enlightenment is that vanishing.

IGNORANCE IS the identification of an image with its own reflection. It is the belief of a piece that it alone is the whole. It is the way of life that follows from the belief that your self-image is real, rather than being a mere figment.

This identification thought is the "ego." It is the sense that we are in fact this particular person or character that in fact is fictional.

Now because the nature of the Self is that it is pure awareness, pure reflection, this identification thought, this ignorance, this *reflection of limitation*, must be a distorted reflection of the unlimited Self in its totality. The pond when still reflects the sky perfectly. To make it reflect something else, you have to stir it up, make waves.

A thought is nothing more than this kind of wave that obscures — or seems to obscure — the Self. The Self is not obscured. It simply is shining down on a moving mind, and so its reflection is muddled. Even that muddled reflection is a perfect reflection — of a sky in muddled water.

As long as the thought waves of partial reality keep arising, the mind reflects such partial reality.

To get to a clear reflection, you need to quiet the mind. A quiet mind is the necessary precondition to the destruction of ignorance and to the seeing of the Self.

IDENTIFICATION-BASED **habits of thought**

What form the chief barriers to this quiet mind are habits of thought, feeling, and desire that are based on the notion that one is an individual, separate self. These generate all kinds of distracting negative emotions and desires. These are the generators of the constant thought waves.

As one attempts to follow the steps in this book, these habits will distract you, often very powerfully. They will attempt to lead you down pathways of greed, lust, and anger that will disturb your mind more and more. The very steps in this book *are* the ways of playing these habits out and changing them, even as these habits are the obstacles to these steps. A sincere attempt will eventually win out over the habits. It is just a matter of patient effort.

The habits do not have to be entirely changed to reach the spiritual goal; they only have to be relatively quieted. As you start to glimpse the Self, that too will further quiet the habits.

THE GREAT DRAMA is that the mind does not want to be quieted. It identifies with itself, and its whole survival is based on that. This requires a continuous stream of new thoughts that distract you from seeing the Self reflected in its purity. So the mind keeps generating desire and fear based on the thought that it is a separate person. As in a dream, it anticipates danger and pleasure and keeps wanting more and new things.

This desire that we chase to be happy seems endless. We go after one thing and then it leads to another and another, and we never get the satisfaction that always seems just over the horizon. This is the great mirage, the Siren, the mystery just around the corner. It is the will o' the wisp, the illusory swamp light that would lead travelers into quicksand. It is the function of the ego to preserve itself this way.

To conquer it, the mind must be quieted. This will involve not giving up all desire, but trying to discern our true desire from our false desire.

When the mind is quieted and realization occurs, the structure of the mind is altered so that the frame around the picture is seen along with the picture. Or if it is a movie, the screen behind the movie is seen.

Actually, the frame and the screen were always in view to the Self. The only thing that changed is that the drawing in the picture or the character in the movie now claims to know it!

The whole ordeal, and life itself, from back to front and left to right, is illusory. If you could believe that totally and completely relax, unconditionally accepting whatever came your way forever, that would be instant enlightenment. Because you cannot do so, you are condemned to seek.

The way we dispel the illusion

So the game is to see through the illusion of personal self-hood. How do we do that? There are two things required: a quiet mind and an investigation of our own experience.

A quiet mind is so critical because of the way the mind functions. The reason we don't seem enlightened to ourselves right now is because we *identify* with our body, our thoughts, our feelings, etc. The way this identification works is that we have inside us the sense that "I am" X — where X is our feelings, memories, relationships, etc.

This "I am" is our identification thought or ego. The identification thought depends on a constant stream of other thoughts to attach itself to in order to distract you. One moment of a truly quiet mind and you would suddenly see the truth. This is because the mind is like a mirror made out of pure awareness. If it is polished, all it reflects is that same pure awareness. When it is dirty or cracked, it reflects parts and pieces. These parts and pieces are identifications with the mind and body.

Clean and fix the mirror, and the identification can't last because the full picture can then be seen. Candlelight cannot be seen when placed next to the sun.

A truly quiet mind requires, most crucially, an investigation of our own experience. The idea is that we are not what we notice. We notice a table; we're not that table. We notice our hand; we're not our hand't.

If we use that principle and trace back the nature of our own experience of ourselves, of our own sense that "I am," we'll find that it — disappears. That disappearance needs to be prolonged. When it is, it eventually yields the clear sight that the mind is just a thought and that we are not the mind. That's the goal.

So, a quiet mind and self-investigation. That's the plan.

PART II

QUIET THE MIND

4

METAPHORIZATION

A quiet mind is crucial to enlightenment.

A quiet mind is a concentrated mind. It is focused on one thing, not many things. This means that it is not easily distracted by a whole bunch of disturbing, unwanted thoughts, feelings, and desires. This is important because the restless movement of the mind distracts us from seeing the truth that is right in front of us, the truth that *is* us. The more the mind bobs and weaves, the harder it is to see on what surface it does its bobbing and weaving. Quiet the mind and the distraction dies down, and we can "see" the underlying medium.

There are two main ways to quiet the mind. The first is to discover and be honest about what we want, and to attempt to fulfill it. The second is to pursue the Self, which is the third step in our overall system. The quiet mind aids in the pursuit of the Self, and the pursuit of the Self results in a quieter mind.

Ultimately, pursuing the Self yields truth, but the experience of perfect bliss and happiness are the results of a quiet mind. A relatively quiet mind leads to the Self, and the realization of the Self over time leads to an almost completely quiet mind.

In this section, then, we will try to figure out how to quiet the mind by being honest with ourselves about what we want.

To be honest about what you want, you have to feel and be familiar with your feelings. Your feelings usually have a bodily components, unlike your thoughts, though the two are often combined.

Your feelings give you critical information about what you want. Simply being aware of your feelings can, all by itself, be useful.

Yet trying to decode their implications can be complex. Two ways of going about this are what I call, respectively, *metaphorization* and the *science of desire*.

Metaphorization follows from our discussion earlier in the book about the Self and its relationship to the individual mind. To try to understand our desire is to realize that the Self, or cosmic mind, is intelligent, and communicates with us through our desires. We cannot make spiritual progress unless we decode these mysteries layer by layer, and in the process uncover the objects of our desires, and appreciate the way we experience life.

For while we desire objects in the outer world, we just as much desire to know the way we see that world. And while both of these are secondary to the pursuit of the Self, they are required for that pursuit, because, again, they quiet the mind. One cannot effectively pursue the Self if one earnestly desires something else and is unaware of that fact.

To understand more deeply what metaphorization is and why it is important, it is necessary to go into a bit of theory about how the mind puts experience together.

IF THERE IS a kind of entity or artist behind the individual mind called the cosmic mind or Self, it is certainly worth learning to communicate with it, or at least to decipher its communications to us. Is there a way we can understand what it is saying?

Every conscious experience we have is a weaving together of data from our sense organs along with our memories and beliefs. Our experience at all times is a unified, seamless fabric. We do not experience it as little bits of sense and feeling and thought stuck together — a desk here, a song there, an emotion somewhere else. We see the desk and hear the song and feel the emotion in one smooth, continuous, connected weightless fluid of awareness or consciousness.

The cosmic mind or intelligence takes the raw flow of sensory information, makes an infinite set of judgments connecting them with the rest of our mind, and then makes an instant decision to surge certain pieces together into a seamlessly-related whole that is greater than the parts, resulting in a moment as unique as a color you see once and never again, a particular taste you savor and which you can never quite fully express.

For the intelligence to carry this activity out, it requires values. What are the nature of these values? How does the intelligence decide, among an infinite number of possibilities, how experience should be assembled?

The answer is that experience is a kind of art. The cosmic mind that creates it is a kind of artist.

It cannot make its decisions on the basis of what is conventionally good or bad. Conventional concepts of good or bad reflect events *within* experience. Yet an artist is beyond the events in the artwork. No one suggests a screen-writer should not write a script in which terrible events happen to good people; those events are happening to fictional characters, so what is good or bad in the world of the script is not the same as what is good or bad in the real world.

So the intelligence cannot be bound by normal notions of good and evil. Yet some sense of value and some sense of intelligent structure must guide it, and we might call that value beauty. The intelligence makes beautiful pictures, and it makes them make sense not only as individual pictures but as a series: as an individual perspective.

THESE VALUE CHOICES manifest uniquely for each person. Each person's unique perspective is the result of the specific combination of decision-making the cosmic mind/intelligence uses to assemble that person's experience. Experience contains the complete set of choices the intelligence makes. It is the artistic structure of the person's view of the world. And nothing in it is accidental. That is what makes experience supremely artistic: the fact that everything in it is there by design. If there are messages communicated to us by the intelligence, they are in the design and intricacy of experience.

The choices of the intelligence have to do with "what it is like" to experience something and therefore "what it is like" to be us. And of course, "what it is like" to experience something can only be expressed in terms of other things it is like or unlike, or things it relates to. In language, when we compare things by resemblance and difference to other things this way, we are using *metaphor* in a broad sense.

The metaphors that come to mind when trying to express experience capture different aspects of the experience.

When a human artist employs metaphor to express the "what it is likeness" of experience, the artwork reveals the embedded judgments made by the cosmic artist in the creation of that experience. The artist's style and viewpoint reflect and discern the intentions of the intelligence. The closer the metaphors used come to the artist's true sense of the experience, the better they reflect those intentions.

My use of metaphor is itself metaphorical. A metaphor need not be a word. It can be anything that is used to convey what something else is like. For example, when someone paints what they have seen, they are, in the first place, saying that what they have seen is *like paint*. The very use of any artistic medium is an immediate first metaphor. But things go far beyond that. When Romeo compares Juliet to the sun, that is a metaphor that expresses his feelings. Beethoven's Ninth Symphony likened the feeling of certain of his experiences (and they could be imagined experiences; they don't have to have actually happened) to a particular structure of sound.

I therefore call the process of trying to express in art what an experience is like "metaphorization." It is by examining our experience and attempting to convey what it is like as closely as we can that we can decode some of what the intelligence has put there for us to appreciate and enjoy. We decode its specific communication.

Most importantly, we learn this way what we *desire*.

The intelligence assembles reality such that some things are interesting. We want them, or want to avoid them, or want to know more about them or to control them. Any topic or person we are passionate about holds messages about what we want that we can plumb through artistic expression.

It is desire that holds the key to what we should be attempting to express if we want to decode the messages that are left for us – and perhaps send some back.

5

METAPHORIZATION: THE NEEM METHOD

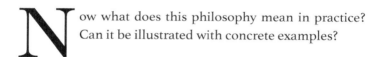ow what does this philosophy mean in practice? Can it be illustrated with concrete examples?

A SHUDDER of pain ran through Jared's leg when it cramped. He gritted his teeth and wondered when this hell would end.

Lisa felt shattered, cold, nauseous, and despairing. Her boyfriend had just cheated on her, and she was still in shock.

As much as he looked around, Sam saw nothing meaningful anywhere. It was all futility, as far as the eye could see.

Barry felt a constant stream of worries: about his job, his health, and, most especially his daughters. These worries ate away at him, and he hated the fact that he had so little power to affect their outcomes.

WHAT IF JARED and Lisa had the power to see beauty in their pain? What if Sam could find meaning in his bleakness? What if Barry had a way of exerting control over his anxieties?

The cramp feels like massive clenched jaws of pain, an army of fire ants sent to gnaw my nerves into pulp, Jared wrote, and suddenly felt better. The pain was still there, but it seemed different.

Before we get to a technique for metaphorization, I want to emphasize how incomplete these examples are. The ways that one can express one's experience are infinite, and the following technique is just *one* of many possible approaches to metaphorization.

What happened? Jared used a simple and powerful method to transform pain into beauty. The same technique can be used to transform *any* experience, including happy ones, into beauty. It can be used to make any experience richer, deeper, and shake out some of the truths that are in it. Most importantly, it quiets the mind.

I CALL my recommended method (again, it's just one possibility) for metaphorization **NEEM**:

    1. Notice your **Experience**
    and
    2. Express it in **Metaphor**

Notice your Experience

Right now, notice what you are:

- Feeling
- Thinking
- Seeing/Hearing/Touching/Smelling/Tasting
- Remembering

- Expecting
- Imagining

Express it in Metaphor

Now take anything you find interesting in that experience and express *what it is like* to experience it.

Do this by *comparing* it to something else. That's the metaphorical part.

Be as ***original*** as you can. Do not just repeat cliches.

Try to capture as ***accurately*** as you can what it feels like to be undergoing your experience.

You *can* use words, but you do not have to.

You can use painting, music, or any other art form which you find comfortable.

If you are not good at art, it doesn't matter. No one needs to know what you make.

If you need to, start out by describing your experience in physical terms ("it is red," "it is round") or simple emotions ("I am angry," "I am irritated").

You are not trying to be a movie camera and get every little detail but to capture the overall *impression* of your experience, the overall sense and feel of it.

But move on to comparing your experience to something more specific. If you feel angry, what is your anger like? Maybe like a landscape, an animal, or a story you've heard? If you feel pain, what is the pain like? Maybe like hammers? What kind of hammer? Be as specific as possible.

What images come to mind when you ask yourself what your experience is like?

Write that or draw that or sing that or play that.

The experience can be of a minute or it can be of a life-

time. Different time periods, different areas of emphasis —
whatever interests you is valid.

Try to convey what you're feeling so that someone else
who sees, reads, or listens to your art would feel it too —
even if that someone else is only an imaginary person in
your mind.

~

Now let's apply the technique to our sufferers. We've
already seen how Jared dealt with his physical pain.

Lisa had just been dumped by her boyfriend. She tried to
focus on what she was feeling and thinking. She felt dizzy,
dazed, dumbfounded. She found herself taking out a sketch-
book and doodling large, lonely landscapes. She drew frost
and ice, because that was what she felt the world was. She
drew her boyfriend sticking a knife into her heart.

And as she drew these things, she felt the world clarify.
She took more of a studied eye to herself. Her experience of
pain became a crystalline object to her, one she was
studying from every facet. And as she drew, her experience
clarified, and as it clarified, her drawing got clearer. It was a
mutual process. As this went on, she started to feel a sense
of peace and beauty.

~

Sam had to deal with his sense of meaninglessness. He took
out his laptop and started writing a short story. It told of a
boy who looked for something interesting, and no matter
how far or how long he looked, he could not find it. He tried

many different things, but they all ended in either disappointment or disaster. Finally he simply sat under a tree and stared into the sunset.

As Sam examined his sense of futility and put it into fiction, he felt as if he had finally bitten into some substantial fruit. There was structure and strangeness in his experience, and he was seeing, it, and himself, though his writing. Through the expression of his meaninglessness, he oddly enough felt a sense of meaning.

BARRY HAD to deal with compulsive worrying. He tried to notice each of his worries: about his daughters, about whether his boss liked his work, about who would win the election. He had always liked playing on his guitar, so for each of these, he composed a little melody. What was it like to worry about his daughters? It reminded him of something both fearful but also nostalgic. He knew he couldn't protect them forever. So he strummed on his guitar, and tried to compose a little ditty that expressed that strange combination of feelings. And he found that as he did so, even though he was no great songwriter, that he seemed to gain perspective. He started to understand what he might like to improve in his relationship with his daughters. There was even something exquisite about his worries, something very personal and unique to them, a Barry-esque way of looking at things. Through his worries snaked an underlying beauty.

THIS, in a nutshell, is metaphorization through the NEEM

technique. You could make things far more complex, and write huge novels or direct award-winning plays to express yourself. And people have. But it could be as simple as the above examples. As you apply NEEM, you will find that you adapt it to your own methods and needs. That is good and necessary.

∼

METAPHORIZATION AND MEANING

Metaphorization deals with the meaning of life by taking the question—and the question of the meaning of *anything* that happens in life—and says: that question is in part a desire for more complete expression of itself. It says: if you express all the desires, emotions, urges, motivations, wonders, doubts, fears, and fantasies that you have about the "meaning of life" or the meaning of your disease, relationship, country, addiction, or of anything else at all in your life, that very process will itself help slake that thirst. And that means a quieter mind.

In the end, however, metaphorization cannot give a full sense of meaning. Only enlightenment can do that. But metaphorization can quiet the mind's need for meaning relatively speaking and enable it to follow the methods of pursuing the Self outlined later in the book.

∼

METAPHORIZATION, pain and messages

The cosmic intelligence which is our Self often brings us to an experience because it has a message for us. That message is always expressible as a work of art. We can use metaphorization to produce that work of art. When we do that, we "get" the message.

We reveal at least some of the important thoughts underlying that experience, and often the Self then moves us on to something different.

So often, metaphorization can cure a pain or a fixation, but not always. When it does not, it often means that there is more than one message to be extracted. Create a more complex work of art, express your experience in a richer manner.

For example, if someone survives a massacre, that is an incredibly powerful and horrifying experience. It may bear an enormous number of messages within it. A single or simple NEEM which results in a few quick thoughts will not cut it. It may require many expressive attempts to fully articulate all that there is in that experience (not to mention how helpful good psychotherapy may be).

Each of these attempts allows you to create a more refined narrative of your own life, to understand your own motivations more clearly. You can, through NEEM, show how you experienced a situation, had certain thoughts and feelings about it, and then acted based on those thoughts and feelings. Your actions then become comprehensible as a sensible narrative to yourself. That can often relieve a lot of pain.

If an experience is powerful, it may generate enough art and opportunities for self-understanding for a lifetime.

IN THE END, the Self/cosmic mind is playing games with us. The spiritual game is just one more of these games, though it is the most important one. All these games proceed by understanding the other player's moves. And that's where metaphorization is our mode of communication. When we metaphorize, via the NEEM method or otherwise, we start to find what it is we truly want and learn to enjoy the beauty hidden in our own way of seeing the world.

Metaphorization feeds into a larger structure that I call the science of desire. Together, they are the key means by which we quiet the mind over time and prepare it for Self-realization.

6

THE SCIENCE OF DESIRE

The science of desire is, as the name suggests, a way of progressively uncovering your desires through a repeated process of hypothesis and testing. There are two ways of doing this. The first is to envision some scenario. For example, let's say you're debating which of several jobs to apply for. You use your imagination to envision, as clearly and in as much detail as possible, what one of these jobs would be like. Then you monitor your feelings and metaphorize/NEEM them. Are they good? If so, and it's clear that you want that job, you could apply for it.

Alternatively, let's suppose your feelings about the scenario did not turn out well. Maybe your metaphorization helps you understand your feelings are complex and conflicted, and that you might want something different. Then you could try envisioning, based on your findings, another scenario to see what that something might be. The metaphorization should give you hints about that next possibility. The whole process takes time and effort, of course. You will often not find the right answer except through repetition.

There's also the important step of testing something in the real world. In addition to envisioning things, you also actually try them out. If you're worried about the city where your new job is, perhaps you try visiting for a few days. Then do the same thing — monitor and express your feelings in original, accurate metaphor.

In this way, you'll get clearer and clearer about what it is you want. As you get clearer about what it is you want, you can pursue it. Both the getting clearer and the pursuit of it will make your mind quieter.

Both envisioning scenarios and testing in the real world ought to be used hand-in-hand with metaphorization to discover what it is you really want (which of course can change over time). Once you know it, pursue it. If you feel a reluctance to pursue it — that's a message. Metaphorize your feelings of resistance. They are simply other desires that need a voice. Metaphorize them and that voice shall be heard. Then attempt to envision new scenarios that give all your voices and values a place.

You cannot fight what you truly desire, nor would you want to. You can only get clearer on just what it is that you desire, so that you don't pursue things that aren't actually what you want. Going after what you really want quiets the mind and prepares the path to enlightenment.

Willpower and conflicting desires

What about willpower? The normal notion of willpower is mostly nonsense. Willpower is simply what happens when what you think you want is aligned with what you actually want. When you know what you want, you then have the stamina to go after it, even through long periods of struggle. That comes from alignment with your true desires.

Your truest desire, of course — and this will become clear when you go down the rabbit hole of clarifying desire long and far enough — is for something eternal and perfect and true: the Self.

What about conflicting desires? Conflicting desires can seem to exist, and they must be progressively clarified through metaphorization and the science of desire. Over time, they will synthesize into something higher that incorporates them all. All these conflicting desires only *seem* to conflict. In fact, they each hold parts of a greater message.

For a while, you may simply need to allow these seemingly disparate vines to climb before they reveal themselves to be part of something connected.

For example, suppose you feel like you really want a cigarette but you also feel bad about having it. Metaphorize both feelings, and see if you can get clarity about why both voices in you want what they want. Perhaps you want the cigarette because it quells your anxiety, and you want to stop because it's bad for your health. Is there another way that you can quell your anxiety? Ask yourself, and use the science of desire to try various solutions until one clicks.

The assumption should always be that conflict *can* be resolved with time and effort. The very fact that you are in conflict suggests that there is a higher, third possibility. You might not be ok giving up the cigarette without another way of feeling calm — and by examining the conflict in detail, you might find out that that is just what you need to do in order to quit. Fortunately, all of these searches are backstopped by the pursuit of the Self, which, when seen clearly, always serves as a final source of peace with respect to any conflict.

In the end, you will learn that you are at peace even when you seem to be at war.

Negative emotions

A similar set of ideas applies to any negative emotion that you might be experiencing and that you'd like to deal with. Any negative emotion is indicative of a desire that needs to be heard and possibly pursued. Commonly, these emotions are encoded with judgments. Anger usually indicates that you feel treated unjustly. Fear means that you think you are in some kind of danger. And so on.

In reality, of course, emotions are not pure and they are often quite complicated. They can hide each other. They can be repressed or altered by psychological defense mechanisms. For example, it may be more tolerable to feel anger at yourself than anger at a loved one.

All these nuances of the desires behind your negative emotions can be extracted through metaphorization and the science of desire. Often such emotions simply require expression and clarification. That *is* their desire: to be heard and understood by you. When they are, they automatically transform.

Sometimes, however, they require action. Hunger cannot be satisfied simply through metaphorization. It requires food. And that may be the case with other negative emotions as well.

But the basic approach is simple: any negative emotion is a message. Find it out.

Alternately, as you'll see later, you can touch the Self, and that will put the emotion in perspective as well. That is another way of handling it, though the two are not mutually exclusive. You can both decode the message behind the emotion and put it in a larger spiritual perspective.

Metaphorization and the science of desire: your personal oracle

Together, metaphorization (NEEM or otherwise) and the science of desire allow you to be your own oracle: you can ask questions of yourself and find answers. And you should.

When you pose a question to yourself, like "Should I go on vacation to the Poconos or to the Caribbean?" you instantly generate a set of emotions and feelings in your mind. If you then take those feelings and express what they are like — say, a kind of warm sensation with the Caribbean when thinking about lounging on the sand, but also a sharp, cold fear that it may be too crowded or expensive — you will grasp your feelings better. You will clarify your thoughts.

Envisioning the scenarios in more detail, taking some practical steps along each route, and metaphorizing at each point will clarify things further and further.

You may not get an answer immediately, but you will see more clearly which questions you should be asking, and what your next step in the decision-making process should be. At every moment, our inner self is sending us messages. If we are unsure of a decision, that uncertainty *is* a message. We need to decode that uncertainty, and metaphorization and the science of desire in combination are the way to do it. Decoding it may require sitting patiently with it for a good while, however.

When we want to listen to our inner voice, or understand our emotions or our selves better, we have a set or toolbox of techniques. We take our feelings about a topic and metaphorize it. Then we test our understanding of our desires against imagined and real actions. Then feel and express again. It's a cycle.

If we have an emotion that we do not understand, we might use metaphor to express what it feels like. "It feels like I've left something undone," one might say, and instantly one knows one's feelings and desires better. This kind of clarification is often just what we need.

To some extent, simply expressing the emotion puts it more in our view and under our control. Often our emotions simply need to be acknowledged, not even fulfilled, before we can move on and receive the next message from the Self. That is not always true, however. Some desires will remain: they either require further expression or they have to be pursued in reality.

Any time we want to commune with a higher power, we have the ability. At any time we can ask a question and then express how we feel immediately after that. Or we can express larger chunks of our life, thinking of our last decade as an answer to the questions we asked ten years ago. And so they are.

In the end, the science of desire and metaphorization are the most powerful ways to quiet the background of mind and prepare it to look inward and realize its true identity — to pursue the Self and to recognize it as the invisible fullness hiding in the obvious.

7

OTHER KEY METHODS

There are two other powerful and recommended ways of resolving questions of desire and quieting the mind.

Psychoanalytic therapy

The first is psychoanalytic therapy. This is not the same as therapy generally. It's a specific kind. It's the method devised by Freud and followed, with variations, by his successors. It holds that each of our unconscious minds is marked by conflicts, often from childhood. If we can see those conflicts better, then instead of them controlling us mechanically, we gain greater freedom to resolve them as we wish. The therapeutic situation provides an environment where these conflicts manifest clearly, often in our interaction with the therapist. While metaphorization is powerful, you usually can't see all your blind spots on your own. There is also the powerful positive healing effect of a supportive and nonjudgmental relationship. If you want psychoanalytic therapy, find your local psychoanalytic institute and ask for a referral. Remember too that not every therapist is a match. If after a couple of sessions you don't feel a rapport and that you're getting something out of the process, try someone else. It can take a few tries to find the right person.

Silence

The second method is simply to sit with a conflict or a confusing emotion or feeling in silence, watching it without getting drawn into it or being negative about it.

Letting it be without judging it will often allow something to arise out of it spontaneously. This is a more traditional spiritual technique than metaphorization and the science of desire. It can be very useful, but it should not be the only tool in your toolbox.

You ultimately have to grow clearer about what you want in order to be more at peace with yourself. All these techniques are not only compatible, they reinforce each other. They grow in power when used together.

Other considerations on the spiritual path: food, sex, etc.

Traditionally, spiritual seekers were instructed to control various aspects of their life in order to better quiet their minds. They were told to eat a pure, mild diet — usually with little oil, few spices, and little or no meat. They were also told to stay away from sex and romantic relationships.

These can be helpful, but they are not necessary. It depends on the person. There are some practical reasons for these suggestions. Food affects our energy levels and mood. Sex and relationships can be a huge distraction, and can make quieting your mind much more difficult.

In the end, however, what matters are your own true desires and temperament. For some people, sexual abstention might cause many more problems than it solves.

There are other little aids that could be useful: yoga, exercise, and various kinds of retreat. These are all optional and whether to use them depends entirely on individual circumstances and personality. If they suit you, if they help you, go right ahead and employ them. If you are curious, experiment. Use metaphorization and the science of desire and see how your inner self responds. It is the first and final spiritual teacher.

&

Doubts about enlightenment

A final important aspect of quieting the mind is clearing doubts about the theory and method of enlightenment. This book's quick summary of these points is sure to raise a host of questions. That is good. These questions must be addressed through your own thinking or by asking a spiritual guide. Any resistance that you feel to the process must be admitted, metaphorized, and tested in various ways to see what it is really saying and how it might be addressed.

It is through these means that progress happens and understanding deepens. Doubt, question, test, repeat.

Ask questions of others, of spiritual teachers, and of yourself. Do not take anybody's word blindly. Think about it and see how it feels. Question mercilessly until you no longer feel the need.

PART III

PURSUE THE SELF

8

SELF-INQUIRY AND SURRENDER

The pursuit of the Self is, you will find in the end, a contradictory idea. You *are* the Self. You cannot pursue what you already are. That said, as a seeker, you must attempt to do just that, and the end of your searching will be to find that you never needed to search.

The pursuit itself boils down to two very simple methods. The first is *self-inquiry*; the second is *surrender*. Usually the first is pursued, and then the second, but the reality, as usual with these things, is that they are intertwined.

They might both be said to be forms of meditation.

Meditation

Meditation really refers to a family of practices that attempt to quiet the mind in order to see the truth. They fall generally into one of two categories. The first is concentration meditation. Here you try to focus the mind, by, for example, chanting a mantra or trying to keep an image in mind.

The second is what's called mindfulness meditation. There you let the mind simply think what it wants, and you observe it without judgment and without getting sucked into any thought. You maintain your status as the "watcher."

The first builds concentration and can soothe and clear the mind.

The second shows you clearly that you are not your thoughts and feelings, and so helps you detach and accept them.

Normal meditative practices of these kinds help quiet the mind, but not permanently. Mental pain and disturbance is ultimately based on the ignorance of our real identity, our notion that we are merely a person. Self-inquiry and surrender are special versions of each type of meditation that cut ignorance at its root.

∼

Self-inquiry

The basic idea of self-inquiry is that the sense that "I am" is literally a kind of hallucination, a trick your mind is playing on itself. Question it correctly and it disappears.

So how do we question it? You feel, right now that "I am reading these words." You feel "I am sitting here" or "I am standing here" or whatever it is you are doing. You feel "I am this body," "I have these thoughts," "I ate that yesterday," "I am named so-and-so," etc.

So this feeling of "I am" — or just the "I" — is like a bright light that's shining. You feel it strongly at all times. It's what seems to be attending to these words right now.

The aim of self-inquiry is to try to trace that feeling of

the "I," to find where it is coming from, to what in your experience you can attribute it.

To trace the "I am" feeling, you have to regard it as a feeling like any other. You know very clearly that "I am." That feeling is *right here*.

Now you are going to try to find it. Imagine there was a sound to your left. If I asked you "where is the sound coming from?" you would respond that it's coming from the left. If I asked you how you knew, you'd trace the feeling to your ears. That's a very concrete tracing of a sensation. A similar thing would happen if I asked you where the piercing feeling was coming from if a needle was piercing your skin. You would locate it exactly.

In the same way, you are going to try to find this "I am" in your body or anywhere else in your experience.

There is one basic rule to this game: you cannot be what it is that you notice. Suppose, for example, you felt that your "I am" was coming from your head, as so many people do. It's somewhere in my brain, you think. But *you've noticed that sensation*. If you notice it, you aren't it. That makes sense, doesn't it? Because you feel "**I'm** noticing this sensation in my head." If you're noticing it, you aren't it. You *think* you are it, but you *can't* be it — the "I am" feeling is still right there, *noticing* the sensation you've just mistakenly identified as it!

So once you notice that, you have to keep looking for the "I am" that noticed that feeling. That I am feeling is extremely clear and unmistakable. Focus on it. Attempt to clarify it into a particular location! The feeling could take many forms. It could be a sensation, but it might also occur to you as an image in your mind, for instance. If you believe the "I" is an image, take your time and notice that "I am aware of this image," and so it can't be the case that the "I" feeling is that image.

If you can't find the "I" feeling in your body, search your feelings, your thoughts, and your memories. But don't search them randomly. Remember, you have the unmistakable sensation of the "I am" right here. Hold it, do not let go of it. Try hard to catch what it is and where it's coming from. And every time you come up with an idea of what it might be, subject it to the test: ask yourself if "I am" noticing it. If you are, keep searching. This may be frustrating. Be patient.

Now I don't want you to get the impression that this is in any way an intellectual exercise. You can read all kinds of spiritual and non-dualistic texts that try to explain intellectually what you actually are. This book has already had many such sections. They can be very valuable. If you need that to quiet your intellectual desire to know and to instill some faith in the spiritual pursuit, by all means read them and think about them. I did.

But this self-inquiry exercise is not that, and it is more crucial than that. It is about finding the source of a feeling that is clear and obvious to you right now.

Above all, hold the feeling, feel the feeling of the "I." If you can't locate it at the moment, just feel it, focus on it, concentrate on it. If you feel your mind going peacefully blank or still, don't allow that to happen. Ask yourself to whom that feeling occurs — "I am" experiencing that blankness, that stillness. Hold the "I."

If you can only do it for ten minutes a day, do it for that long, but eventually, try to do it longer and longer, and in various places and while you are doing other things. The ideal is to do it at all waking moments.

HERE IS what is going to happen. If you try in earnest to find this sensation somewhere in the landscape of your experience, if you try to figure out where in your body it might be coming from, or where in your thoughts, etc. — at a certain point, something interesting is going to happen.

First, as already suggested, your mind is going to get quite still. This is the result of your concentration on a single thought — the "I am" thought. Concentration results in stillness. But if you hold on to the feeling of the "I" that is experiencing that stillness and stubbornly continue trying to localize it, that feeling of the "I am" is suddenly going to vanish. It will be unmistakable when it does.

The Spacious Mind

What will replace it is something I like to call the "spacious mind." It is going to be a sense of vastness and peace. There will still be awareness, but you will not feel the "I am" identification that you are used to.

You might feel that what you thought was your little individual I actually turns out to be the entire world, somehow. You might feel that what you thought was yourself seems like somebody else, a third person, and that that person lives *within* that new strange sense of self, a sense of self that does not feel like "I."

This new self will feel vast, solid, and completely fulfilled and satisfied in some deep way.

This is the state you're aiming for. If you've ever been in a state of flow — of effortless, optimal performance — when playing music or in athletics or in any other demanding activity, this is that state. The spacious mind is actually the truth of your nature, only you don't quite recognize it yet. It is a state where you don't feel like you do not feel like you are the "doer" of activities. That burden is lifted.

Almost as soon as you get to the spacious mind you will lose it. What can be lost and gained is not the Self, but the spacious mind is helping you glimpse that the "I am" feeling, shockingly, despite its clarity, might actually be an illusion. Look deeply enough into it and it disappears, to be replaced by a Self that doesn't feel like "I." In the spacious mind, you no longer feel like the doer.

Once you fall out of the spacious mind, always because some habit of thought and identification jars you out of it, immediately self-inquire again and get back to it. This very effort is quieting your mind, and your other efforts to quiet the mind (like becoming more honest about your desires) will help you too.

You will find that it takes less and less effort to get to the spacious mind over time. Eventually, you won't need to go through the whole process. You'll just say a word and think a thought and there you'll be, just about.

You can do this whole process sitting down in a quiet area, but you can also do it walking around or working. With a little practice, you can and should do this as close to constantly as you can.

But how can you do this while you are working, you might wonder. The truth is that you only ask the question because you've misidentified with the small mind and body, the doing self. Attempt self-inquiry even in the midst of your work and you will see that with some practice it can be done, and that it does not interfere.

Surrender

But even this is going to be frustrating, because it requires too much effort. The tedium will tear at you. You'll wish it was more automatic.

And this is the value of surrender. For in truth, the "I" doesn't exist. The sense that "I am" and the sense that "I do" are the same sense, and it is that sense of doership that causes fatigue and problems with decisions and so on. That sense of doership is completely false. You aren't a person, you aren't yourself, you aren't the one who chooses *either* to act *or* not to act.

You aren't a you.

So what are you? Well, you are that which is effortlessly, utterly quiet and is simply the space in which all these occurrences occur. Now, you can't force yourself to feel that way, but what you can do is to surrender.

When at a certain point you feel the desire to stop the self-inquiry, simply attempt to let go. What does that mean? It means allowing everything to happen as it does. Just allow whatever happens to happen. Drop your habit of thinking and of worrying about past or future. If thoughts happen to occur, don't think about that either. To the extent you're able, just let all the reins go. Allow negative or positive emotions to happen without comment.

This is a practice too — and it *is* effort. It is not complete surrender. It is the seeker's surrender. Still, it is less effort than self-inquiry. Usually you won't be able to attempt surrender until you've followed self-inquiry for a while, but if this path appeals to you from the start, go for it. But whatever happens, you've got to let go: even if whatever is happening is terribly unpleasant. Even if you are complaining bitterly about it, let that go. Don't exert any effort to change anything about your own reactions or the situation. Don't lift a finger to *deliberately* engage the mind. If thoughts flit across your mind spontaneously, that's fine. If actions happen spontaneously, that's fine.

Note that this does not mean you deliberately should lie on a bed and do nothing. You should allow action or inaction to happen spontaneously. If you spontaneously lie on a bed and do nothing, fine, but you are not aiming for anything in particular. Give up all aims.

All this is mimicking or aligning the mind with the real state of affairs. You feel you're lost but you're actually right at home; with surrender you're pretending that you're at home, which will eventually help you realize that fact.

Now note that there is one thing you don't surrender, and that is surrender itself. You *are* putting in the effort to relax, to avoid holding on to anything, to grasping at anything. The mind *is* engaged with that one task. You *are* putting in effort to not get involved in your thoughts. In that sense there will be a feeling that "I am surrendering."

If you do stray, if you do exert effort, if you do worry, if you do think deliberately (you will do all of these things), don't compound the error by worrying about it or scolding yourself. Let it go.

Surrender will also lead you to the spacious mind, just as self-inquiry did. And you will drop out of that state and then go back to it, over and over. Your lengths of stay in that state will lengthen, however.

Allow that to happen, putting as little effort into thinking about it as possible. Relax. Just allow whatever happens to happen, doing whatever you do as if you're in a dream.

States of mind

At this point, a word about states of mind. The key to the pursuit of the Self is the right state of mind. That state is the quiet state. Over the course of the book, you've seen many methods to deal with various obstacles to mental quiet. In this one, we've been talking about how self-inquiry and surrender deepen that quiet.

In a sense, this entire book is about achieving mental quiet. Mental quiet is our true identity, but the kind of mental quiet I'm talking about is not incompatible with thought.

It might be helpful at this point to distinguish between various mental states, and their relationship to the mirage of individual identity that we are trying to dispel.

Unconsciousness

The state of unconsciousness is exactly what it sounds like: it is what we experience in deep sleep or after we've fainted and so on. We still exist. Our minds still exist. It is simply that we are experiencing the complete absence of thought, perception, and sense of self.

Dream

In dream, we have internal perceptions, thoughts, feelings, and a sense of self. From our waking standpoint, this seems like a distorted and often inconsistent sense of self in a world that does not seem to follow sensible rules. But that is from our waking standpoint.

WAKING

This is of course our normal state. Perception, thought, feeling, and our sense of self are active as usual. Depending on how focused or quiet our mind is, the thoughts and feelings come in more or less frequently, in more or less disarray.

STILLNESS OF MIND

This is a first and extremely important mental landmark. This is that state of mind you get when you are deeply absorbed in something, when you are not experiencing any thoughts — or, to be precise, when you are completely absorbed in one thought. You have forgotten yourself. It is a state of seeming blankness. How do we achieve this state? There are several ways.

First, there is the method of concentration. This is focusing on any one idea to the exclusion of all others. It includes the concentration meditation we talked about earlier and also the method of self-inquiry.

Second, there is the path of relaxation. This is about not focusing on any one idea, but rather on on *not* getting drawn into any one idea. It includes the mindfulness meditation we talked about earlier and also the method of surrender.

There are also many accidental ways we enter this state in daily life. We might get absorbed in some particular idea without even intending to do so. The world gets blocked out, we lose all notion of ourselves, and we experience stillness.

Or we might relax some moment, laying on our back looking up at the stars, and the mind goes limp, and we naturally relax and "zone out." We might go into a kind of pleasant trance when driving or doing some other repetitive activity as well.

Psychoactive drugs as well as hypnosis can also cause alterations in consciousness that lead to a temporarily thought-free state, though they may or may not be spiritually helpful.

THE SPACIOUS MIND

We've already described the spacious mind, but there's a bit more to be said about it.

While stillness of mind can be very pleasant, it is not the goal. Indeed, if you let yourself simply coast there, you could zone out for a long while. This is called a meditative sleep, or "yoga nidra" in old-fashioned Hindu parlance. It is relaxing, but it is not spiritually productive. It does not destroy the habits of identification that keep you in ignorance.

What has to be done is to keep a still mind with a certain continuing intent, that is, a subtle underlying thought — either to continue self-inquiry (by holding the feeling of the "I") or to continue to surrender. In other words, don't lose the stillness by falling into the normal waking state, and don't simply fall into the pleasant bliss of zoning out. You might ask if surrender is compatible with a continuing intent. It is. Surrender means not grasping, and here it means not grasping the blissful quietness of thought that is so tempting.

If you keep awake with intent even through the stillness, you will eventually enter the already-mentioned spacious mind. This is a mental stillness that is not sleep and that is in fact compatible with an underlying intent.

Stay there, and, when dropped out of that state, get back

to it via self-inquiry or surrender, again and again. At some point, something beyond what your mind is able to conceive will pull you in.

The realization

As self-inquiry and surrender are in full swing, the mind will grow quieter and quieter. You will spend more and more time in the spacious mind, but not quite all of the time.

At a certain point, you will simply glance at your mind, and you will realize that what you thought was yourself was clearly just an image, a somebody else. Actually, you will have many such realizations, flashes and glimpses of the Truth that you will not be able to maintain fully.

At some point, however, this realization will sear into you like lightning, will strike you with the force of total clarity. It will be unforgettable and seem blindingly obvious.

That's the realization we're aiming at. It will simultaneously become screamingly clear just what the Self is: it's the unthinkable unsayable phone tone running beneath and in and through everything, but that is not a thing. You are that. You are also not that, because there is no you. You will see how there is both a difference between it and everything else — and that there is no such difference. For it is beyond opposites.

You will understand clearly that you cannot see it directly but that you *are* it, and that it is a very special kind of thing (though it is not a thing). It is that which knows itself by itself. If you wish to notice it, you have only to pause your mind and the Silence — is that. You will grasp this truth. And you will grasp the paradox of this realization. For *who* realizes this, when the realization is that there is no one who can say "I am" or "I realize"? You will realize that there has been no seeker, no quest, and no enlightenment. But you can't take this on faith or as a logical argument: experience it for yourself.

Note that I haven't mentioned any great out-of-body experience, any great fireworks or ecstasy or miracles or surges of energy. All these experiences, which might well happen to you, are just experiences. They come and go. They are not integral to realization. The Self is precisely that which does *not* come and go. It is eternal and unbroken.

The Self is that which constantly knows itself, and whose knowing can only *seemingly* be veiled by the mind's thoughts, and in particular the mind's identification thought.

It is only a seeming veiling because it is the Self which observes even that veil. The Self is the knower of the entire world and the mind too. And it 'knows' even ignorance itself, even the mind's identification with the mind. And it 'knows' it when the mind realizes its own shallowness and that ignorance vanishes. The identification thought itself then becomes but another thought, once here, now gone. The thought that the mind is real disappears. Realization is the realization that the seeker never existed.

CONCLUSION

You may think the journey is over once the Self has been recognized, but when that has happened, you will know it is not. You will, however, immediately realize why it is said that the Self is the source of happiness, peace, joy, and truth.

Two great tasks remain. The first is that the deep knowledge of Self that has been acquired has to penetrate fully into the mental system. Yes, the mind continues to exist despite the fact that it is no longer taken to be real. It is much like knowing for sure that the Earth revolves around the Sun, but still seeing the Sun seeming to rise and set. The illusion persists despite knowledge.

That is because the old habits of mind and thought still remain, though they will be defanged. Still, they will run around like chickens with their heads cut off, getting slower and slower over time. Self-realization is the most powerful way to quiet the mind, and so the mind will grow gradually more confident in a restful state. A quiet mind is a happy mind. In the light of Self your whole personality will bloom into stillness, and this blooming will take the rest of your life.

The second great thing is that having solved the mystery of the Self does not mean that all the mysteries of life have been solved. They remain. All the mysteries of philosophy, art, literature, and science remain. They are not voided by the discovery of the true Self. There is a realm where those mysteries don't apply. That Truth will have been seen. That doesn't negate the realm where they do apply. Duality and non-duality co-exist, much as the movie and the movie screen co-exist. Further explorations are made by the mind, the one with which you no longer identify. The mind will continue, but without the idea that you are it and it is you — or, if you prefer, *with* that idea but you won't *identify* with that idea!

The ego or identification thought functions in a formal way but is "burnt."

There are new voyages to be had, and you will continue to experience life in all its complexity. Only now, no matter what happens, even in seeming anger and pain and misfortune, you will be at home in the Self.

This book has been but a quick sketch of the spiritual search. I hope it helps you see through the illusion from which you think you are suffering, and see what it is that you already are and always have been.

Understand the theory, quiet the mind through the discovery and fulfillment of its true desires, and pursue the Self. Let these three legs reinforce each other. If you do that and possess a sincere desire for liberation and a willingness to think for yourself, you will attain your goal.

AFTERWORD: MY EXPERIENCE

After twenty years of seeking, of learning to forge principles from the Hindu mystical school of Vedanta, other traditions, psychoanalysis, literature, and philosophy into weapons and instruments that helped me climb each new step,

I did and did not come to the end of my spiritual journey.

I did and did not find what I was looking for.

I found that the one who was searching had never existed. I found that the quest was imaginary, but that its object was real.

For the great, infinitely small, infinitely large, infinitely solid, infinitely empty, non-thing non-person presence-absence behind and in and through all — shone clear at last.

Yet it had always shone clearly. Even in its obscurity and hiddenness, it had shone clearly. Even before it had been recognized, it had been recognized in its non-recognizability.

"I" did not find That, for the one who could say "I found That" did not find it.

So who found it?

No One found it.

Yet No One did not need to find that. No One could not find that. One can only find what one has lost, and No One cannot lose itself. No One ever did.

So what happened?

The structure of the mind altered so that the frame behind it came to be seen clearly. The space in which it existed and which had always existed, and which is and is not awareness, and which is and is not being, came clearly into focus. To whom?

The reflection of that space became clear. To whom?

One can only say that the mind became clearly aware of the boundaries of the mind, and learned in the presence of its own limitations to grow quiet, and to trust. And in that trust and faith inspired by awe, the background became foreground. To whom?

One can only say: all realization — to the extent that it is a *change that happens* — is certainly in and of the mind, though it is not *to the person that the mind thought it was*.

It is a change in the fabric of the mind, yet it is all about, at a certain point, an experience that is beyond the mind. Beyond the mind and of the mind.

Language gets tangled in paradox. Yet it is a very simple thing. It is not supernatural, it is not other-worldly. It is the simple truth of existence.

And yet it is utterly psychedelic, completely mind-blowing. Crazy. Insane. It's the insanity that has always been right here, the endlessly falling backwards, the bass tone underlying everything and in which and from which all objects appear. It is hidden in plain sight, completely self-effacing.

In knowing it one knows oneself to be the uninterrupted bliss of absolute absence.

There are no flashing colors or lights. There are no hallucinations or delusions. I had no great "death experience," as many respected others have. There was simply the observation, a profound click, of seeing, clearly and emphatically, that what had thought itself to be me was in fact a mere image with as much depth as the sky in a puddle.

Yet I was never that me; and that me cannot see. There is no me and there is no you, no not-me and no not-you. And yet there is all those things too.

The realm of the beyond-duality: that realm is so beyond the duality of "I as opposed to the world" that it is not incompatible *with* that duality. It is so purely happiness that in it, even unhappiness is a kind of bliss. It is so purely awareness that it is aware even of unawareness. It is so purely being that it is the being of even not-being.

Yet it is not a thing, it is not a realm, and it is most certainly knowable, more certain than certainty itself — and just as certainly completely unsayable, as incapable of being mentally comprehended. And yet I am talking about it right now.

It is known not through the mind but through itself, a self-shining light, a subject with itself as its own object, the lidless eye that sees itself without having to look at anything outside.

Within it the mind operates. The mind can only see, at most, the limits of the mind, not the medium in which it floats like some strange nocturnal light-reflecting sea creature, lonely and yet utterly connected, a great womb held on all sides, suspended in the abyssal depths.

The apparatus of mind still functions, permanently changed, yet not destroyed. All the mysteries of life, save one, remain just as mysterious as before, and just as worth seeking out, though the seeker is seen to be merely a thought.

The one mystery solved turns out to be not a mystery at all, but that which is absolutely self-evident and beyond mystery.

It is beautiful, it is cool, it is strange, it is none of these things. It is hysterically funny.

It is highly recommended.

Find the Self. All the words are merely pointers.

And yet seekers require them. Take the pointers that resonate with you and follow them.

ACKNOWLEDGMENTS

This book could not have been written without my many mentors and counselors over the years, my friends, and my family. Thank you.

ABOUT THE AUTHOR

Akilesh Ayyar is a spiritual teacher, writer, and speaker. He advocates for a new road to enlightenment based on blending eastern mysticism with principles from philosophy, psychoanalysis, and literature. He has studied and practiced in the Hindu mystical system of Advaita Vedanta for over 20 years and co-authored a book on it entitled *Irreverent Spiritual Questions* with Hindu monk and spiritual leader Swami Bodhananda Saraswati. He has graduate degrees in the law from Harvard Law School, in Information Systems Management from Carnegie-Mellon University, and in forensic clinical psychology from the City University of New York. He has published essays and short stories in *Philosophy Now, The Millions, Lines of Flight, Literate Sunday*, and elsewhere.

Find out more about his ideas and activities
www.siftingtothetruth.com

Printed in Great Britain
by Amazon

41877043R00078